LEARNING TO LIKE MUKTUK

Learning to Like Muktuk

AN UNLIKELY EXPLORER
IN TERRITORIAL ALASKA

Penelope S. Easton

Penelope S. Easton (signature)

Oregon State University Press
Corvallis

The paper in this book meets the guidelines for permanence and durability of the Committee on Production Guidelines for Book Longevity of the Council on Library Resources and the minimum requirements of the American National Standard for Permanence of Paper for Printed Library Materials Z39.48-1984.

The complete *Food Resources of Alaska* pamphlet is available for download on *Learning to Like Muktuk*'s web page at www.osupress.oregonstate.edu.

Library of Congress Cataloging-in-Publication Data

Easton, Penelope S., author.
    Learning to like muktuk : an unlikely explorer in territorial Alaska / Penelope S. Easton.
        p. ; cm.
    Includes bibliographical references.
    ISBN 978-0-87071-758-1 (trade pbk. : alk. paper)
    I. Title.
    [DNLM: 1. Dietetics–Alaska–Personal Narratives. 2. Food Habits–ethnology–Alaska–Personal Narratives. 3. Indians, North American–Alaska–Personal Narratives. WB 400]
    RA601
    613.209798–dc23
                        2014031808

First published in 2014 by Oregon State University Press
Printed in the United States of America

Oregon State University Press
121 The Valley Library
Corvallis OR 97331-4501
541-737-3166 • fax 541-737-3170
www.osupress.oregonstate.edu

This book is dedicated to all Alaskans
who shared their wit and wisdom with me.

Contents

Preface

Learning to Like Muktuk tells of my journey as a dietary consultant in the Territory of Alaska in the forgotten period between World War II and statehood in 1959. As a dietitian, I was an unlikely explorer, and the study of foodways was an unusual pursuit, but for people interested in that vast land and its Native food cultures, my experiences are true adventures. When I mention having lived in Alaska, I continually meet some of the millions of people who have visited there and want to talk about the beauty of the place. Curiosity about the foodways is often couched in a question such as, "Did the Eskimos really live on blubber?" Then I explain that a better word for blubber is *muktuk,* strips of whale flesh attached to black shiny skin, a delicacy whether eaten hot or cold. During my journey I learned to like muktuk and to love the territory in the process.

I have been asked why, after all these years, I decided to write about the many "Alaskas" I knew. Because of my continued interest in the change from territory to the state of Alaska, the public's fascination with our forty-ninth state, and the current emphasis of health professionals on the value of homegrown produce, I wanted to document my eyewitness account of the wealth and value of indigenous foods and Native foodways and lifestyles.

In 2011, on my eighty-eighth birthday, I decided to stop dyeing my hair, publish a mini-book of my verses, and write about my experiences in Territorial Alaska. As I organized and culled many years' accumulation of my papers stored in cardboard boxes, dozens of thin yellow onion skin copies kept surfacing. Because I never learned to type, and had poor handwriting and meager spelling skills, Mrs. Mary Davis, the Nutrition Unit secretary, transcribed my reports and correspondence. When the Nutrition Unit of the Territorial Department of Health was downsized in 1950, I was the last nutritionist left, and Mary helped me rescue those yellow papers from becoming trash. The reports and personal notes have survived haphazard treatment; they have been stuffed in with other professional papers through many moves spanning more than six decades and are now the primary resource for this book.

Among the tissue copies were stories about Native foodways written by schoolchildren in the North. I saved those, too, but I never read them until I started writing *Learning to Like Muktuk*. Mr. Wilson of the Barrow Day School had sent copies of stories to Christine Heller that had been published in their school newspaper, *Arctic Cubs*. I have quoted from the schoolchildren's comments on Mr. Wilson's innovative use of Native foods in the school lunch program. The children also wrote vivid descriptions of the whale harvest I went to in 1949 and the nalukatuk (blanket toss) customs. Because these are valuable historical documents, I have sent the complete packet of Barrow Day School stories to George Harcharek, mayor of the City of Barrow.

Published documentation of food cultures in the territory appeared to stop in 1945 and did not pick up again until after the push for statehood. The years I spent in Alaska were a time of social upheaval. The disruption of village life was catastrophic for Native people, particularly in the interior and Arctic areas, because of raging epidemics of tuberculosis and measles. Patients, even young children, were flown to large hospitals thousands of miles from their homes. The loss of hunters and gatherers in the villages in which the people depended on food from the land was devastating. Children's homes were established because the number of orphaned children overwhelmed the Native tradition of tribal members caring for their own young and ill. As a dietary consultant, my primary focus was on the food served in the hospitals, orphanages, and schools, but since the community nurses were my contact people and arranged my schedules, I became involved in all areas of nutrition.

I am a Vermonter by birth and proud to have been raised in the independent spirit that is part of my birthright. My parents moved to Craftsbury five years before I was born, and Dad was called "the new doctor" the rest of his life. They were active members of the community, yet did continue to have the *Boston Globe* delivered. It came by train to St. Johnsbury a day late. They imported clams and lobster. We also ate lamb, not typically served in the region. Dad loved gardening and grew all manner of flowers and vegetables. We had a family farm, as was the custom: up to six cows and one pig, chickens and pigeons.

The town was justifiably proud of its fine one-room schools and its scholarly academy. The community expected that many of its young people would complete advanced degrees and explore the world beyond Vermont's borders. When I graduated first in my high school class of sixteen, I used my scholarship and worked my way through the University of Vermont cleaning chemistry labs, washing toilets, and babysitting.

After earning my bachelor's degree, I was accepted into an Army dietetic internship at Brooke General Hospital in San Antonio, Texas. Many young Craftsbury men, including four of my brothers, were in military service, so my active duty in the Army Medical Corps came as no surprise to my community. I was in basic training when the war ended and was fortunate enough to get an overseas assignment to be the only dietitian at a general hospital in Karachi, then India. We cared for the flight crews that had "flown the hump" and other personnel from the China-Burma-India theater. My overseas assignment lasted only eight months because of the Indian/British Revolution, but it allowed me to fly all over India and circle the world on troopships with stops in Egypt going over and the Philippines coming back.

My stateside assignment was to return to Brooke General and become the sole dietitian at the small mental health unit, but after a few months, orders sent me to be the only dietitian in another small hospital at Maxwell Field, Alabama, the home of the Army Air Corps. Pilots flew training missions all over the United States, and often I and other ground personnel were invited to go along. After discharge, I spent four months working as the chief dietitian at the New England Hospital for Women and Children near Boston. When I was unable to get a job in public health without a graduate degree and unable to get the degree without experience, the University of Michigan School of Public Health took me as a master's candidate.

My knowledge of how small towns weathered the Great Depression and how the people in them, with their local governing systems, found innovative ways to solve problems and care for all the citizens was the best possible preparation for my work in Alaska. Having observed different lifestyles and foodways in so much of the world, I unwittingly was getting ready for the vast and exciting Arctic land. I was already used to faraway assignments. My old green army footlockers were repacked, taken to the Railway Express office twelve miles away in Hardwick, Vermont, and I booked flights to discover the Territory of Alaska.

When I arrived in Alaska, I, like everyone else, brought my own personal foodway, which included the foods I learned to eat during the Depression years in Vermont, the unusual dishes my parents liked, and my lifelong struggles with weight. After all these years, I realize that my weight problems may have benefited me as much as they distressed me. My brothers were all thin and handsome, and my parents were equally so. I accepted the prevailing opinion that I was the ugly duckling with no chance of becoming a swan. I was the only fat child in town and had to use wits and humor to succeed; my wits and humor helped me survive and succeed in the territory.

I knew very little about the history of the territory when I signed my employment contract. I knew that it was a vast storehouse of valuable minerals and a rich source of fish, game, and furs. I had no knowledge of the migrations of people from Russia between 16,000 and 10,000 BCE who came across what was then the Bering land bridge. These migrants hunted in the Arctic region before they settled. I remembered that Alaska was called Seward's Folly when William Seward, Lincoln's Secretary of State, purchased it from Russia. I was aware of Russian influences. I had heard of the gold rushes in the Yukon and Southeast and of the small cities and settlements that had grown up near the mines. I knew trade and tourism had grown after World War II.

Other aspects of Alaskan history and geography, such as the impact of explorers and adventurers, the devastation caused by the epidemics, and the effects of the war became obvious to me when I visited the different areas of the territory. There was no better way to understand the original groups hunting game in frigid weather than to look at the frozen tundra beneath the wings of an airplane taking me to an isolated village and imagine what it must have been like to walk across those thousands of miles of whiteness buffeted by storms.

I was aware that different groups of people lived in different areas with varying climates. Although in today's world the terms used to identify the broad categories of inhabitants may seem pejorative, the four groups were commonly called: Whitemen, Eskimos, Indians, and Aleuts. I did not know that the earliest immigrants, over thousands of years, had belonged to four distinct groups according to their location, language, and food patterns. The groups consist of Tlingit, Tsimshian, and Haida in the Southeast; Aleut, Alutiiq, and Yup'ik in the Aleutian Islands and coastal southwestern Alaska; Athabascan in the interior; and Inupiaq in the North and on the northwestern coast. The Inupiat and Yup'ik dialects are two of the Inuit family of languages spoken by the northern Natives of Alaska. I never heard the term "Inuit" used to identify people.

Although using the four categories to group all the Native peoples may appear to be insensitive in today's world, I have retained the practice that we used at the time in this book. In some instances, I have added some specific tribal names for clarification. This grouping points up the lack of attention and appreciation by white people of the cultural differences among the more than two hundred different tribes that existed.

I was used to normal business practices, such as titles for people with whom I worked and being called "Miss" after "Lieutenant" no longer applied. The Native people were not given such honorific titles, which helped to separate the races. I had little social and work contact with people of different races before I went to Alaska and I followed the mores of the time without question.

I have used the names of people and the details of our relationships as they were recorded in my reports. In some cases, I did not record names or recorded only the last names. I have tried to locate some of the people mentioned but have not been successful. Few Native people are named because before my return trips, I knew them only as employees, patients, and members of groups and classes.

The Aleut Evacuation, the most important tragedy of World War II for Alaskans, was never mentioned in my first years there. I did not learn about it until I returned in 1996. The Japanese shelled Unalaska and occupied Kiska and Attu in June 1942. In an effort to protect islanders from further Japanese invasions, the US military evacuated nearly one thousand Aleuts, including those from the Pribilof Islands of St. George and St. Paul, from their villages on barely a moment's notice. They were sent in packed ships into deplorable living conditions in internment camps in southeastern Alaska. In a later trip I learned, as well, about an older tragedy. In 1882 the US Navy bombarded Angoon. It thought the Native people, grieving a leader's death, were rioting. Awareness of these episodes helped me understand why white people and their government were not trusted in the villages during the time I worked there. The incidents were part of the history of Alaska I never knew.

Throughout this book, I have used my professional organization's preferred spelling, "dietitian." I also use, as do all other dietitians, the word "diet" to mean "food eaten." Diets for special conditions have modifiers such as reducing, bland, or liquid. The American Dietetic Association, founded in 1917, now the Academy of Dietetics and Nutrition, had rigid academic and clinical experience standards for membership. I have been a member since 1945.

When, in 1950, I found that my travel funds would be so severely decreased that I couldn't do good work in the field, I felt I had to leave the territory. I knew it was necessary to be in the villages and hospitals and orphanages in order to focus on their needs. Letters from my office in Juneau would not suffice.

I returned to Alaska four times between 1996 and 2005, courtesy of a former graduate student, Janell Smith, who dared to ask me to be part of her research teams. I enjoyed taking part in research conducted through methods that respected and involved subjects. As an older person, I was able to know the Native people of all ages and enjoy their wisdom and zest for life, accompanied by their hope and humor. I saw many changes in the foodways and the remarkable retention of some aspects of the Native cultures that I feared had been destroyed.

Recently my grandson, Travis, just graduated from medical school, asked, "Did you make an impact?" I had no answer. A teacher rarely knows what legacy she leaves. My Alaska experiences have enriched my life, and the stories of them have enlivened my classes over the years. I think, hope that something I did, said, or wrote helped Native children appreciate the value of their foodways and the wisdom of their ancestors. I hope as well that I helped the non-Native Alaskans appreciate the Native food customs.

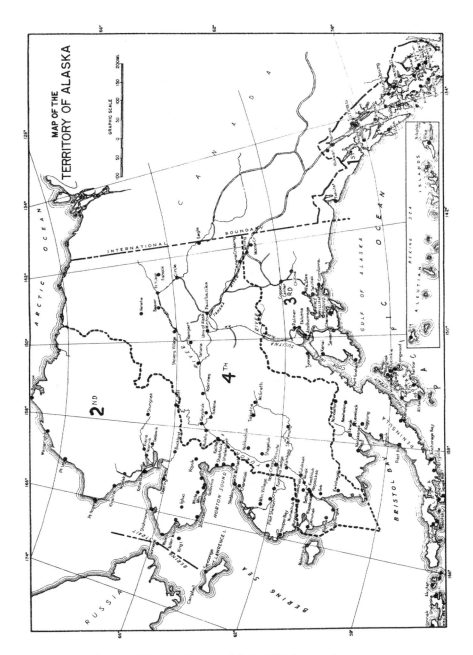

Territory of Alaska, centerfold of *Food Resources of Alaska,* 1950. Source unknown.

CHAPTER 1
Juneau, Home Base

Trains and mail deliveries punctuate life in some places, but in Juneau, it was ships. A shrill whistle was heard, and someone would look up and say, "Guess one of the Princess ships is about to sail. There's the fifteen-minute whistle." One night as I watched the beautiful *George Washington* creep out of the harbor, I realized that of all the ports I had visited on troop ships, none could rival the beauty of this almost constantly misty harbor near the Mendenhall glacier, which fed icebergs into the ocean, their blue-white ice glowing in the rare sun and moonlight.

The harbor was a wonderful backdrop for the beginning of my journey to discover Alaskans and their food cultures. My decision to come to the territory was made in March 1948, four months before I arrived. Dr. C. Earl Albrecht, director of the Alaska Territorial Department of Health, came to the University of Michigan to interview candidates who were graduating with a master's degree in public health nutrition. He persuaded half the class, Helen Amos and me, to accept positions in Alaska. Helen took the post of a traditional public health nutritionist serving the southeast region. Dr. Albrecht was a great salesman and convinced me to take the position of dietary consultant, which meant I had to go farther north than I had ever been. Although I hated the cold weather both in Ann Arbor and Vermont and was considering a position in Hawaii, I agreed to go to Alaska. My reason was not altruistic, but because of the salary he offered. I was not tempted by dogsleds, big game, or the unexplored wilderness, but by money. After struggling through graduate school on the G.I. Bill, the salary of nearly $100 a week looked enormous.

The early days in Juneau were vital to my understanding of Alaska and the agencies that were important to my job. I needed this time to learn about the health department personnel and their philosophical and educational tenets. Dr. Albrecht was the territory's first full-time health commissioner (1945-56). He had practiced in Matanuska Valley until he became post surgeon and commanding officer at the 183rd Station Hospital at Fort Richardson. He was committed to stemming the tide of the tuberculosis epidemic rampant in the territory. His charm had served him well in obtaining federal funds to build hospitals, convincing talented people to work for him, and attracting worldwide attention for use of the latest treatments for the disease.

In my first days of discovering Alaska's capital city, I met other government workers who, like me, were seasoned by the Depression and war years. Helen Amos, my Michigan classmate, arrived in Juneau several weeks before me, and when I got there, we learned about our new home together. We had many adventures in the long hours of summer light. As in any small city in the territory, everyone talked to us. The ratio of men to women was reported to be seven to one, and Helen and I met many men, young and old. We assumed that every man was married until proven otherwise, just as we did in the Army. We learned not to ask too many questions about past lives because this was a land of new beginnings for all of us, and who you were at the moment was all that was important.

Miss Christine Heller, the chief nutritionist, came to Alaska in 1945 after work as a public health nutritionist in California and New Mexico. Christine was a brilliant botanist and in the short time she had been at the health department had started important research of the dietary patterns of Native groups. She was busy with research, writing books and pamphlets about indigenous foods, when her two new assistants arrived. She provided the guidance that led to the passion of my whole Alaskan experience, the preservation of respect for the sophisticated adaptation of the Native groups to the bounty of this vast, often inhospitable land. She left at the end of my first year on the job to pursue a PhD degree at Case Western Reserve University and later returned to Alaska to become a world-renowned authority on the dietary intake of Native people and the nutritive contributions of Alaskan foods.

Christine did not conduct formal orientation sessions for me, but gave advice and counsel as I learned about the goals of the health department and other agencies that might ask for my services. On my first day in the office, she tested me to see if I had the quality she considered essential to the work of the unit, good food manners. "Miss Easton, if you can't sit on a dirt floor and eat anything that your fingers find in the common bowl, go home."

I was delighted to receive this challenge. I knew the importance of respecting others' food habits and hospitality. I had swallowed a raw oyster at an elegant party in Palm Beach and eaten grits for breakfast in Virginia. In Karachi I risked dysentery, against orders not to consume dairy products, to eat ice cream from a gold bowl during a Festival of Lights celebration. I even ate Aunt Bertha's baked beans. As a young second lieutenant, I took a bus from Maxwell Field, Alabama, in ninety-eight degree heat to visit my aunt fifty miles away. Aunt Bertha greeted me warmly and said, "I have cooked Boston baked beans so you will have a taste of home."

All my life I hated baked beans. If I had had to eat them to survive, I would have been svelte. I took as small a serving as possible, spread it around on the Wedgewood plate, and ate several bites to show how much I appreciated her effort. I said they smelled like the ones Mother made. Three months later I repeated the trip, and she repeated the menu. This time Aunt Bertha greeted me with, "You enjoyed the beans so much, I made them again!" I was glad to know that my new supervisor and I were in sync about using good food manners and assured her I was staying.

Joy in my new situation was lessened when two weeks after my arrival, my brother called to tell me that my father was in the hospital. The family hadn't phoned sooner because they didn't want to worry me and did not perceive the seriousness of his disorder. Dad, a 1904 graduate of Harvard Medical School, was a real country doctor. He had wanted me, his only daughter and youngest child, to be a nurse. He enjoyed my professional training and appreciated that my expertise was as great as that of a nurse when I became an Army Medical Department dietitian based in Karachi. On my infrequent home leaves, he asked me to prescribe diets for his patients. The morning I left for Alaska, he had taken me to the bus in Burlington.

Dad always wanted to go to Alaska and promised that he would visit me within a year.

My heart was warmed when person after person, new acquaintances all, offered money for me to travel home. Since I did not feel I could afford to go so far so soon, I stayed at my job. When Dad died two days after the phone call, these new friends chartered a boat to take me out to the sea. There was no fog that day, and the sun allowed me to grieve in the beauty of the harbor.

I became more convinced that I had made a good career choice as each day passed. Helen and I continued our informal explorations. We met business people and engineers, and Helen made a friend who lived at the Baranof Hotel and owned a recreational fishing boat. No one told us about the original Native inhabitants in the Juneau area. We heard a lot about the gold rush days but didn't ask about the Tlingit Indians who had settled the land thousands of years before. We were only vaguely conscious of their descendants, who lived in what was called "the Native section."

The men from the gold rush era were called "sourdoughs." As the gold mines closed, they became tourist guides for the multitude of cruise ships, worked in the fishing industry, or just enjoyed being old-timers. Some enthusiastic younger people, who came for adventure and stayed to work in the fishing industry or commerce, also identified themselves as sourdoughs. On my first trip to the Lower 48 in 1949, I even described myself as one. It had such a mysterious ring to it, and I couldn't resist embellishing my experiences a bit.

Juneau's status as the capital city was being challenged because it is not at the center of the territory and far removed from the interior. Such challenges continue to this day. Many homes and office buildings clung to the sides of the mountains amid some fifteen miles of roads and probably more miles of wooden stairs, which served as sidewalks. Every place I lived in Juneau required climbing steps. There were ninety-three steps between my apartment and our office, but I never felt tired from the climbing, and the exercise did not make me thin.

I lived in a series of sublet apartments until I shared a small house with Helen and two other government workers. The house had no hot running water but was otherwise well equipped for our needs.

Helen's friend at the Baranof Hotel was a generous man and allowed us to troop over to his room for hot showers and welcome shampoos.

The Nutrition Unit was housed in three rooms on the corner of a bank building apart from other territorial offices. This allowed Christine, our chief nutritionist, to enforce her strict policies concerning colds. She insisted that at the slightest hint of a cold, we must stay home because no one was indispensable and no one should be allowed to contaminate another's space. In my last months in Juneau, I had a more personal reason to appreciate isolated office space because a florist delivered a single flower to me every Friday afternoon. My admirer's government salary allowed for only one flower a week, but it was always a perfect one.

The size of the population of the territory, 100,000, was easy for me to visualize because the football stadium at the University of Michigan held a few more than that. I could "see" the number of Saturday fans spread over 424 million acres of land and water. The breakdown by race was approximately 50,000 white people, 25,000 Indians, and the rest were Eskimos and Aleuts.

More than fifty government agencies were responsible for territorial affairs. The US Department of the Interior was the principal federal agency over the Department of Health. It included the Bureau of Indian Affairs component that was called the Alaska Native Service (ANS).

On August 10, 1948, Dr. Albrecht and Miss Heller sent a letter announcing my arrival to twenty-one ANS Hospitals, twenty-six children's homes, all the public health and ANS nurses, ANS day schools, and administrative personnel in territorial departments of education and welfare, as well as the ANS medical and educational divisions. The letter said:

> Miss Easton will be prepared to help with food budget problems, food order problems, storage problems, menu planning, food service, therapeutic diets, cook and kitchen help training, and the demonstration of such food products as dehydrated vegetables, dried eggs, high nutritive bread, etc. Requests for her services can be made by writing directly to the Nutrition Unit of the Territorial Dept. of Health.

The job description also said that I was expected to provide any nutrition services requested by health personnel and to contact institutions run by religious groups and local governments when I was in an area.

When I examined the announcement, I knew that I was prepared for each of the tasks, but in the aggregate they did seem daunting, as if I could remake the world. I assumed that any water I was supposed to walk on would be frozen. There was no mention of furthering appreciation for the Native food cultures, which would rapidly become my passion.

I knew about hunting for rabbits to feed a family of seven or more, how to preserve garden peas, and how to make crabapple jelly. My time as a dietetic intern with the Army and on active military duty taught me how to order food, instruct people on how to cook in quantities, and adapt menus for patients. Although the post-war years had brought more food and better distribution of it, the habits of frugality remained with me. To this day, I have trouble throwing away used but clean aluminum foil.

Because there were no written procedures for filing reports or referral forms at the health department, I needed to devise my own systems of reporting. I sent informal reports describing food supply crises, lesson plans, and descriptions of people I met as well as results of my field trips, including some of my adventures, back to the Nutrition Unit for typing. Semiannual and annual reports went to the appropriate divisions, as did pleas for emergency supplies desperately needed at the institutions I visited. No office ever acknowledged receiving any of my reports. I suspected then, and am surer now, that no person in power read them, but I am grateful for those tissue copies, which have followed me all these years.

I was surprised to discover the prevailing attitudes of many of the professional people toward educational philosophy for Native cultures. Under the leadership of Dr. Sheldon Jackson the segregation polices were strict and cruel. He advocated that children be completely separated from their tribal cultures and family ties. Dr. Jackson was appointed the first General Agent of Education in Alaska in 1885, a position he kept until 1907. Sheldon Jackson had many years of missionary experience with the Indians in the Lower 48 and founded numerous schools there, as well as schools for Native children in Alaska. He believed it was necessary for white people to civilize Native "savages," to teach them English, and to convert them to Christianity.

Dr. Jackson's philosophy concerning food cultures taught the children to be ashamed of their tribal roots and to embrace only the Whitemen's lifestyles, including their foodways. Teachers were instructed that children should speak only English, even in the village schools. On one of my trips back to Alaska, a Yup'ik Elder with a PhD told me how he got his name, George. The village schoolteacher lined up a group of boys and gave them all English names like George, Henry, or Walter. No use of their Native names was allowed, even at play. Jackson's educational philosophy was still followed and enforced in many institutions in 1948.

A few weeks after I arrived, my understanding of the health and educational climate of Juneau and the Southeast was enhanced by a quick trip to the Mount Edgecumbe boarding school and adjoining hospital in Sitka. The school and hospital, recently built on a deserted World War II installation and administered by the Bureau of Indian Affairs, was considered a state-of-the-art facility. Great attention was paid to sanitation because of the large number of tuberculosis patients. The dietitians, two of the few professional ones in the territory, were concerned about the popularity of the foods they served; they had observed that food acceptance improved after the children knew the nurses better. I was surprised that the food they were most concerned about was reindeer meat, usually a popular item for Native children. Later, I realized that I should have asked about the home villages of the patients and where the hospital got the reindeer meat and how was it cooked.

School was not yet in session, but as I visited with the home economics teacher, I could tell she had been taught and was complying with the English immersion philosophy originally advocated by Sheldon Jackson. She proudly showed me her new laboratory, equipped with coal and wood ranges to teach girls the use of both kinds of stoves. She also had plans for home management houses, one to be what she called very simple, with only one bedroom, and the other a more ideal structure that would include a nursery. I didn't comment but I felt that what she considered "more ideal" was hardly relevant for the Native children who lived in the northern rural villages where children were cared for by all members of the family and having a room just for children was a foreign concept.

The girls' matron at the school told me she wanted a table set for the staff in the dining room so that the children could observe gracious family dining. She felt that the staff had to eat in the dining room to maintain discipline, but she wanted them to have their table set with tablecloths and nice dishes while the children ate out of enamel bowls and cups on a bare wood table. I suggested that perhaps the children would be uncomfortable and resentful about the stark differences between serving styles. When I found she was determined to follow her plan, I proposed the children be invited to the table a few at a time so that they could converse with older people and learn about dining etiquette firsthand. My suggestion fell on deaf ears.

I was beginning to see that educators judged the lifeways of the Native tribes as inferior, even barbaric. That attitude influenced all aspects of the children's care and education. I was not used to thinking of people as second-class citizens. In Vermont, the people who worked on our family farm or in the house were called hired men or hired girls and shared our family meals and living spaces.

When I met graduates of Mount Edgecumbe in 2001, I became aware of the extent of harsh discipline and mistreatment of some of the Native children and the bigotry that had been directed toward them. These graduates had advanced educations and had become important Native leaders. They told me they still carried psychological scars from being abused and treated as inferior in their formative years.

Not far from Mount Edgecumbe, the Board of National Missions of the Presbyterian Church operated Sheldon Jackson High School, the oldest school in Alaska. It started as a vocational school for Native children. The principal showed me the campus, including the newly decorated dining room. He said that the students did all of the cooking except for what the dietitian did. I disapproved of a professional dietitian being a full-time cook, but I kept my mouth shut.

Mount Edgecumbe's main problem was lack of money. The current budget of thirty-six cents per student per day was inadequate.

The dietitian had hopes of getting it raised. She said the diet was low in protein and the incidence of anemia was high. The children had large quantities of reconstituted dry skim milk to drink, but local hunting and fishing did not furnish enough meat to make the diet adequate for growing children.

Before I left Sitka, I visited Sheldon Jackson Museum, the oldest concrete building in Alaska. It housed Dr. Jackson's extensive accumulation of Native artifacts collected from the whole territory. I found an irony in his efforts to preserve the treasures of the very tribes whose lifeways he was dedicated to destroying.

My public health classes had prepared me well for understanding epidemics in populations without immunity for diseases brought by outsiders, and my orientation time brought this into sharp focus. For more than a century, Native Alaskans had been victims of small-pox, influenza, typhoid fever, respiratory diseases, and the rampant tuberculosis and measles. I was not familiar with the methods of care for victims, especially the young. Traditionally, people who lived from the bounty of the land cared for their orphaned children, but these diseases had devastated whole villages, including otherwise healthy adults who would have taken care of the children. Many white people came to Alaska to treat victims of the diseases that other white people had brought.

Most of the children's homes that housed orphaned Native children were run by religious orders. Since my family had not been members of any church, I had no experience with the missionary movements that so influenced the education of hundreds of children.

When I was a child of ten, Mother told me about a meeting of the Women's Missionary Society at our local Congregational church. Although Mother was not a member of the Society, she had gone to a meeting where the group was filling what they called the "Missionary Barrel" as requested by a foreign mission in Africa. Mother came home incensed that the list for much needed supplies included twelve damask dinner napkins. She could not fathom that church people in Africa would ask for such luxuries from a small New England church still struggling from the Depression. I had no doubt that the Alaskan missions I visited over a decade later were considered "foreign" to the societies that sponsored them and filled similar requests. The staffs of these missions wanted to show the Natives "gracious dining," but it was both impractical and cruel.

The missionaries who endorsed the prevailing educational philosophy were not bad people, but they were convinced, as was Sheldon Jackson, that it was necessary to prepare Native people to live as Christian white people lived. These zealots didn't realize how the Whitemen's own culture could be enhanced with preservation of Native ways and how living from the land was valuable as a way to subsist in Alaska. They didn't understand that Native languages and foodways could coexist with those of the white culture. Many, but not all, refused to let the children speak their tribal languages, thus preventing them from communicating with their own Elders. I learned how this practice, as well as the loss of Elders from epidemics, nearly destroyed the traditional knowledge system of teaching the younger members of the tribe how to exist from the land and to be proud of their ancestors and their own advanced culture.

The loss of hunters and gatherers to the epidemics of measles and tuberculosis and war-related activities extended the near famine conditions in the interior. By February, called the "Starvation Month" by Native people, the seal pokes (storage bags made from intact seal skins), which were filled with greens and berries, and the stores of dried or frozen meats and fish were usually depleted, especially if there had been a poor hunting season for caribou, seals, and whales. Each year some residents died of starvation, and in many areas symptoms of severe malnutrition could be observed.

Early explorers discounted Native knowledge, and lack of respect for Native wisdom was still common in 1948. The explorer and anthropologist Vilhjálmur Stefansson observed in the 1920s that the Eskimos suffered no ill effects from a very low carbohydrate diet and that sufficient vitamin C was obtained from raw meat and whale skin. Stefansson's recommendation that an all-meat diet was healthy aroused great controversy among vegetarians, dietitians, and nutritionists. Local lore told that Stefansson refused to believe his Native guide, who had cautioned him that polar bear livers were poisonous. Despite the warnings, both the men and the dogs of his teams ate the tender livers. All showed some of the ill effects of hypervitaminosis A: nausea, vomiting, muscle weakness, headache, high blood pressure, damage to the kidneys and heart, and, in the extreme, death. Even if the story was apocryphal, later research has shown that polar bear livers do contain toxic amounts of vitamin A.

Although some local people in the Juneau area picked berries, most newcomers didn't make good use of Alaska's greens and berries. During Vermont springs, my father had urged the gathering of wild plants such as dandelion greens or fern fronds, largely overlooked by local people. These greens were cheap and provided valuable sources of nutrients not readily available in the winter. I had no idea that consumption of such foods in Alaska would be scorned and ridiculed by settlers.

My first experience with the wonderful berries occurred when a friend shared some thimbleberries that he said grew wild in the area. Native people cherished and used the abundance of salmonberries, blueberries, and highbush and lowbush cranberries. Christine introduced me to goose tongue, nettles, wild celery, dock, and fireweed. No matter where she was, if she spotted a green plant, she stopped the car to gather samples to test and to eat, if edible.

I learned about the Native methods of preserving foods: the drying and smoking of fish, especially salmon; the preserving of berries in seal pokes; and the use of cold cellars dug in the permafrost. When meat and fish were plentiful, Native people consumed large portions. Berries and greens that were harvested in the summer and stored in sufficient quantities kept the people from starvation. Hunters and gatherers in the villages gave shares of all harvested food to the young, old, and ill. My orientation to Native foodways included information about the eating patterns that I was likely to find in villages, such as a communal stew or soup pot kept hot and available all day with no distinct meal times. Meats and fish were eaten completely, stomach contents, entrails and all, supplying valuable and scarce nutrients.

Rosehips were a great surprise. Although it was probably true that the tiny seedpods on our old-fashioned roses in Vermont were rich in vitamin C, we never suspected it. Somehow the Natives discovered the curative values of the huge red-orange seedpods of Alaska roses. Children often ate rosehips directly from the plants as they ran through the countryside in the fall. Jellies or purees made from rosehips went a long way in preventing deficiencies in vitamin C for hundreds, maybe even thousands of Alaskans. I included copies of 1947 health department rosehip recipes with the educational materials I planned to take to the interior in the fall.

Livers from fish and other animals were an important part of the Native foodways. The willingness of white people to discount the high level of Native sophistication was still evident in the post war, pre-statehood years. I was surprised to learn that the most important food from the sea was seal, not whale. Seal oil is to Alaska Native foodways what olive oil is to Italian cuisine. In a seal poke, seal oil was poured over the food to prevent it from spoiling. A seal poke was made from butchered seal with the skin of the flippers and head tied off and left intact. The pokes were used for storage of berries, greens, and fish in seal oil. For preservation, the poke was hung in a cool place. Meat and fish were often dipped in seal oil.

I was not fond of seal oil at first. It usually had an odor because it had been stored for months. In the northern regions, seal oil was made with the oil dripping from the blubber. The strong flavor was partially due to small particles of meat left in the fat. In the southern regions, the seal oil was rendered with heat and was crystal clear and

Pen and ink drawing of polar bear and seal on ice floes, by Junior Tingook, acquired 1950. Easton Collection.

delicate. Seal meat was usually boiled in a stew and tasted much like whale or walrus. Its texture was firm and somewhat fibrous, with fat concentrated directly under the skin. All parts of the seal were used, some for food and some of the skin for clothing.

Whale meat was important in the diet of Eskimos, and I learned to call blubber *muktuk*. There were different phonetic spellings of muktuk, but the definition remained the same. Muktuk is strips of whale skin with a small amount of fat, or blubber, attached. Like in seals, whale fat is concentrated below the skin. Muktuk is eaten raw or boiled. Whale meat has little marbling in it. The successful harvest of a whale often ensured that members of a whole village would not starve before spring.

Christine introduced me to Multi-Purpose Food (MPF). The soy-based product was designed to cure starvation throughout the world: Alaska was one of the 129 "countries" that received MPF to prevent malnutrition and famine. The blue and white one-and-a-quarter pound cans needed no refrigeration; two ounces of the powder furnished a high protein meal for three to five cents. The ingredients were lima beans, soy grits, potatoes, cabbage, parsley, tomatoes, onions, leeks, and seasonings.

Each hospital and orphanage had been offered the opportunity to buy MPF. In my field visits, I checked for the presence and use of MPF and found little enthusiasm for the product. Some institutions had a supply on hand but didn't use it. Others had occasionally made soup with it, and although staff said the children liked it, they discontinued its use. The price seemed low to promoters, but a serving of MPF could have taken ten percent of the daily monetary allowance for a child. I tested MPF in cookie recipes, as well as in soup and stew and demonstrated MPF products at the public health nurses' conference in Anchorage in 1949. I never found recipes that appealed to me. My conclusion was that it was not "real" food, and I found the odor and amount of spices in the mix unpleasant. Native Alaskans liked bland foods and the flavor of slowly cooked meats. Probably advising MPF as a possible emergency food caused no harm, but it certainly did not solve the need for more and better food supplies.

The prevailing foodways I encountered my first summer, including my own, were typical for New England or the Midwest, fresh fruits and vegetables in season and frozen or canned in winter months. These foods were available in Juneau and other southeast areas because of year-round boat and barge deliveries from Seattle and Portland. We government workers usually ate meat, mostly beef, and potatoes once a day. We ate cereal or toast and eggs for breakfast, and sandwiches for lunch. The food was more expensive than I was used to, but my income was higher as well. We sometimes ate steaks, but more often we had soups, stews, spaghetti and meatballs, or casseroles made with ground beef. We included canned vegetables and such fruits as peaches and pears in our meals, always canned in thick syrup. We opened the cans with the small hand can openers that left jagged edges waiting to grab careless fingers. Our desserts were puddings, pies, or cakes.

A welcome change in my diet was fresh salmon steaks from the day's catch. Our Baranof Hotel benefactor who allowed us to shower in his room also made it possible for me to catch my first salmon on his boat. I was forced to clean and fillet the fish, but becoming acquainted with really fresh salmon made the cleaning worth the effort. Salmon fresh from the sea spoiled me forever for the canned product. My acquaintance with salmon while living in Vermont had been limited to the dreaded pink variety we thought suitable only for cats. After the Depression, improved financial conditions at home meant we could have canned red salmon, which we made into loaves, patties, or creamed with canned green peas. Foolishly, I, like most everyone else who ate canned salmon, had discarded the soft bones instead of crushing them as Native people did and thus benefiting from the calcium that they furnished.

Many longtime residents, not new government contractors like me, were great outdoor people and made good use of clams, crabs and mussels, cod, flounder, red snapper, ducks and geese, and venison, moose, and bear. Many cookbooks were available, published by churches and community organizations. They provided non-Native ways of preparing and serving the local bounty.

While I had been used to baking bread in Vermont, my new friends' romance with sourdough starter was somewhat of a nuisance. The gold seekers had brought sourdough starter to Alaska; it was precious during the gold rush days. Although not a purist about starting mine from yeast spores swirling in the air, I kept a sourdough starter pot in our communal refrigerator, religiously adding the pre-scribed ingredients at dictated times. I decided that keeping up with the sourdough starter was as much trouble as a husband. As a single woman, the truth of my observation was open to question. Sour-dough products were popular in communities near old gold mining camps and became a tourist attraction in the whole territory.

The thousands of tourists who came to Alaska annually exceeded the number of residents, but their experiences did not extend to Native foodways. The cruise ships had elaborate menus, and the passengers didn't taste Native foods during their short stops ashore. Travelers on the *S.S. Baranof* in early May, 1950, were offered one fish item for each meal—Alaskan salmon, cod, or halibut—but there was no evidence that any of this fish came from Alaska. When tour-ists were told about Native food habits such as eating the whole fish, they were appalled, yet fried whole smelt was one of the choices on the ship's menu, as was scrambled calf's brains on toast. The wisdom of the Native food cultures and appreciation of Alaskan food groups would have added to the visitors' experiences and fostered apprecia-tion of Native adaptation to the beautiful but often harsh land.

At first, I, like the other stateside-trained medical personnel, looked at food service operations in the local institutions with the eyes of a white person. When Christine took me to visit the Juneau Indian Hospital, the director of nurses and the physician expressed interest in the nutritional aspects of the patients' welfare. The nurse asked for help with the menus, especially for the evening meal. I took the menus back to the office, evaluated them for specific nutrients, and found them adequate, but low in vitamin C, vitamin A, and iron. I gave the nurse some recipes and suggested moving some desserts to the small supper meals. I never asked about the foodways of the people for whom the hospital was named, didn't talk to any patients or find out if their cultural needs were being met. I studied the food service procedures as a well-trained dietitian would. My advice prob-ably was as good as any of the moment, but it lacked knowledge of and respect for the lifestyles and traditions of the patients. Christine taught me much about practical public health nutrition and told me, "Don't let that shiny new degree show. You will gain respect for what you do, not your degrees. Anyway, you will learn far more than you will ever teach."

Each trip, whether for pleasure or business, increased my knowledge of my new home. Like almost everyone else, I learned to like the restful rain and mist, welcome the infrequent sun, and find each day exciting. I realized what Juneauites meant when they said fog was soothing and too much sun wore them out. After one heavy rain, Gold Creek was dangerously high, and the rocks churning in it could be heard for some distance. I was at the hospital next to it, and it certainly roared. I did not tire of the blue glaciers, the fogged harbor, or the ships' whistles announcing another voyage. Yet I was eager to visit the cities to the southeast that appeared to cling to the mountains to escape falling into the sea.

CHAPTER 2
Alaska's Panhandle, Doorway to the Lower 48

The September sun had shone for two days in a row. Helen Amos and I strolled all Sunday afternoon to enjoy every ray of sunshine. The autumn days were much shorter by then; still, at 8:30 p.m. we had bright sunlight. The miles of wooden stairs and the shoreline activities at Juneau never ceased to interest us. One evening we saw the motor ship *Hygiene* in dock, ready to go north. I knew that after a trip to the Southeast, I, too, would head north and explore different parts of the territory.

My first real field trip was to the Southeast, the area from Ketchikan northwest through Juneau to Sitka, also called the panhandle. Not part of the peninsula of Alaska, the panhandle is separated from Canadian British Columbia by the northern part of the Pacific Mountain system. The inhabited communities grew up around inlets, small islands, and narrows. Transportation between towns was possible only by air or water. The unique rain-forest climate of the southeastern coast has made it a favorite tourist destination. The warm summers and the rich glacial silt facilitate lush gardens, providing growing seasons for an abundance of wild berries and greens that attract deer, moose, and bear. The warm water in shallow eddies and bays yields clams, crabs, scallops, cockles, and mussels and hosts a multitude of migrating ducks and geese in spring and summer. I always loved the oft-used description, "The cities in the Southeast look as though the mountains are pushing them into the ocean."

This trip was intended to be more orientation for me, but it also turned out to be a fascinating introduction to the panhandle's long history with Russian explorers and missionaries and the effects of recovery from World War II. The panhandle was so close to the Lower

48 that there seemed to be little or no demarcation. I learned a great deal from the public health nurses who were my allies, teachers, and village contacts about the problems of hospitals in small villages and the need for nutrition education. But I learned almost nothing about the Native people. I did not ask enough questions or closely observe the Native culture. When I returned many years later, I took the opportunity to appreciate the members of the Tlingit and Haida tribes, who have been leaders to the growth of Native leadership and pride.

The morning after our Sunday stroll, with my usual promptness, I walked the short distance from the office and arrived at the Alaska Coastal dock at ten o'clock. I had weighed in what I described as "all I owned" in a Val-pack (a zippered, canvas garment bag) and "all I knew" in a briefcase. These plus the hard-sided overnight case brought me up to fifteen pounds of excess baggage. I was not able to determine whether what I owned or what I knew had tipped the scales to that great weight, but these items accompanied me for the next two years. I settled myself down for half an hour of waiting and watching the activities of a floatplane office. To my surprise, one of the men from the health department administration office came to see me off. The sunshine was enough to entice anyone to leave work and get outside. I had been told that before the health department got so big, a holiday was granted whenever Old Sol appeared after the usual grey mist and rain.

At 10:15, the man at the desk showed us down to the dock, saying the plane was ready, but it wasn't. Instead, a tiny plane that had been stored above the dock had to be brought down on an apparatus known as a "submerger" before the plane I was taking could be loaded. It was fun to see them pull this little puddle-jumper around, load it, and send it off. The desk clerk spent a great deal of time listening to the radio, the principal communication device. As on our Vermont telephones, everyone listened in and sent along personal messages like, "John says he can't meet Eric and Peter because he is waiting for machinery" or "Mrs. Johnson says to tell her husband she is well and not to worry." The doctors prescribed by radio, and I soon found that the operators knew the health department personnel schedules. I was intrigued the first time I heard my own name:

Author waiting for floatplane to Southeast, 1948. Easton Collection

"Miss Easton is not going to Dillingham today but should be getting there next week."

After rechecking the radio and making sure that the small plane had gone, the clerk gathered the passengers' luggage and helped me walk on the wobbling gangplank to the door of our floatplane. To compensate for the sunshine, a strong wind started to blow. The airline personnel declared it to be a baby Taku. I had been told that in Juneau Taku winds came from the northeast in the fall. They could be violent enough to shatter windows and knock people down. This storm was strong enough to make our trip bumpy, but we took off, and I was glad Petersburg was only an hour away. Suddenly we put down on the water in what seemed to be the middle of nowhere. A little boat with two passengers putt-putted out to meet us.

As we rode the waves, a fellow passenger volunteered the information that this stop was the Hoad Bay logging camp, a Seventh Day Adventist organization. I heard my first comment of the trip about conflicting foodways. He said that the camp offered good pay and good living conditions, but they couldn't keep help because they allowed no pork to be served on the island. I thought that this religion had other dietary restrictions than pork, for the only Seventh Day

Adventists I had known had been vegetarians and did not drink coffee. I was sure that for Alaskans, coffee would have been a bigger sacrifice than pork, but I kept quiet.

When we landed at Petersburg, Miss Florence Binsley, the public health nurse, met the plane. I smiled, explained who I was, and said how glad I was for the welcome. She laughed and said the welcome was not planned. She was just seeing a little Native girl off to Wrangell, but like every community nurse I met, Florence graciously took care of me. We government workers were often asked to escort children, even very young ones, on various forms of public transportation. Once I was entrusted with a toddler to take on a four-hour trip. I remember how she clung to me but didn't cry when I handed her to the medical personnel, also strangers, who came for her. After seeing some of the really good care children received in the interior, I wondered if the medical care was sufficient reason to relocate the tiny patient and what long-term effects this experience might have caused. We were constantly aware of the disruption the epidemic of tuberculosis caused in the lives of children. Even babies, too young to talk, were often sent to hospitals thousands of miles away from their families.

Florence and I were immediately on a first name basis. She told me how happy she was with her post. She had lived in Detroit and Cleveland but was raised in a small town and loved to devise her own amusements. I was struck with the fact that those of us from small towns had a great advantage in adjusting to Alaska.

Petersburg was a welcoming little city. We couldn't get a cab so we left my big bag to retrieve later, and I carried my briefcase to the hotel. My room was not elegant, but the bed had clean sheets. I didn't have to worry about losing anything in the closet because there was none. Later I unpacked and hung my meager wardrobe on hooks on the wall. A drizzle started, so I felt at home in terms of weather, but the slower pace and small town surroundings were different from Juneau.

As I unpacked at Petersburg, I thought about how different this trip would be from my orientation trip to Sitka weeks before. Petersburg had been incorporated in 1910, and the white population was made up mainly of people of Scandinavian descent. Once the fish canneries opened, they were in constant operation. Native people moved to live and work in the city year round. We called the Native people of the panhandle "Indians" and did not differentiate between the different tribes, Tlingit, Haida, and Tsimshian. I was barely aware of these people who had been the original settlers of this fertile, fish-rich area. I don't even remember seeing their descendants on the streets.

I was amazed at the number of cars in Petersburg. The road extended twelve miles in one direction, three to four miles in the other. Cars, many quite new, went up and down the only street all the time. Petersburg was reputed to be the richest town per capita in the world. I could see that fishing must be a good business, and residents of "Little Norway" must be very good at it. The affluent status of the residents was not reflected in the clothes the people wore. I was glad to see the more casual dress and social informality. I had worn what I considered an appropriate professional outfit: blouse, skirt, hat, and heels, and the nurses were similarly dressed. The affluence of the area did show in the many nice homes, most of them newly painted. The better food and medical care available fostered a lower tuberculosis rate than in most parts of the territory.

Because of Florence's good community relations in Petersburg and her knowledge and interest in nutrition, I had my first opportunity to be a true dietary consultant. The health department and the hospital physician had good communication about patients, especially those on special diets. The ten-bed city hospital, which had been a private home, was spotlessly clean. I was used to similar hospitals because the one in Hardwick, Vermont, where my father practiced, had been such a building. I had not paid much attention to the food service but remembered how hard it had been to get patients up the winding stairs to the second floor operating room.

For nineteen years, the chief nurse at Petersburg Hospital had been on duty twenty-four hours a day, seven days a week. Even in this affluent city, money for the hospital was a major problem. She was concerned about the high food cost of $700 for August. The city council required the hospital to buy all food locally at retail prices. I agreed to send her information on places to order food in wholesale quantities in the hope that she could convince the council of possible savings. We talked about the use of canned evaporated milk because it was cheaper and the locally produced fresh milk was not pasteurized. I grew up drinking non-pasteurized milk without any problems, but was well aware of the dangers of milk-borne diseases. I sent recipes and other information to help her economize.

The doctor needed simple diet instructions for what we dietitians called regular hospital diets, soft, bland, or liquid. He also asked for dietary advice in the treatment of diseases. He wanted to give directions to the cook and to the patients when they were discharged. Thus began the diet manual project that I completed just before I left the territory. I adapted some instructions from the Army diet manual I carried with me, and the hospital's secretary typed them while I was there. I made no mention of cultural foodways of the various Native patients nor did I adjust the instructions for varying economic conditions. I corrected those omissions when the *Diet Manual for Alaskan Hospitals* was published a year later.

The doctor asked Florence and me to visit several of his patients. As I expected, she had the cases well in hand, but it gave me a wonderful opportunity to meet local people. We talked to a nursing mother who was concerned about her baby's rate of growth and a twelve-year-old girl who weighed 165 pounds. The girl was currently working for her board while attending school. She had gained the extra weight while cooking on her father's fishing boat since she was nine years old. The father had not seemed to think that his daughter was too young to cook for a fishing boat crew. Since the doctor, nurse, and the people for whom she was working were all concerned about improving her health and controlling her weight, there seemed to be a good chance that she would be successful. Florence set up a system for having all special diet patients referred to the health department upon discharge, just as the new mothers were at the time. She also reminded them that Helen Amos, my Michigan classmate and the public health nutritionist serving the southeast region, would be coming from time to time and could help follow up on patients.

I met many of the schoolteachers, the Red Cross chairman, and the superintendent of schools. On the only clear night, four of the teachers, Florence, and I walked out to Sandy Branch, a part of

Tongass National Forest, for a picnic. The new kindergarten teacher had been pretty discouraged with the weather until she saw her first Alaska moon that night with us. She was so awed that she began to think she would like her new job after all.

After three days with no flights out of Petersburg, I was lucky to find a pilot who was able to take off and sneak into Wrangell between showers. Wrangell was such a contrast to Petersburg. The two places were about the same size, but Wrangell was far less prosperous. The chief industry, the sawmill, was closed and in receivership. Florence had prepared me for this and said that I had been fortunate to be so well cared for in her hometown. She warned me that because there were no bellhops in Alaska except at the Baranof in Juneau, I would have to carry my own bags to my room at Wrangell's Arctic Hotel.

The cab driver deposited my bags in the lobby. I felt exactly like the heroine in a Western movie. There was no one at the desk, only a pile of keys. The lobby was full of smoke. About twenty men were loafing and talking. The minute the cab driver left my luggage, there was dead silence, and it remained that way for the ten minutes I stood at the desk. I thought the men were looking at me, but I didn't turn around to see. No Gene Autry-like hero rode up on his charger. The ten minutes seemed like an eternity, but finally a clerk came, dug a key out of the pile, and said he guessed the room was empty. I picked up my briefcase and overnight case and said meekly, "I'll come back for the big one." Florence was wrong. The clerk, clutching the key to what he guessed was an empty room, carried it for me.

The room had a new pink rug, orange curtains hiding the clothes hooks, and a clean pink bedspread. The fire escape was an ineffectual looking rope tied beneath the lone window. I decided it might hold long enough for me to get to the ground in an emergency. I figured out why the hotel was named "Arctic"—from the temperature of the water. I was grateful to Florence for having invited me to her apartment in Petersburg for meals, baths, and a shampoo.

In Wrangell, as in Petersburg, I found much in common with the public health nurse, Miss Anne Buckley, who came from upstate New York, went to Michigan, class of '38, and was also an Army veteran. Already I understood that the public health nurses were the most important contacts I would make. They knew their communities and all of the inhabitants. Anne had made arrangements for me to meet the chief nurse and area physician who ran the eight-bed hospital. The staff was discouraged about the hospital's large debt. The city council had found it a burden to run the hospital, even though the services were sorely needed. The town was not interested in helping with the finances because the Episcopal Church had started the hospital and had then closed it when St. Phillips mission no longer had a pastor. Recently the Reverend Hugh Hall and his family had arrived, and the mission was active again. Rev. Hall was now chairman of the hospital board and eager to see the hospital recover financially.

As in Petersburg, the town of Wrangell wanted all the hospital food to be locally bought. There were only two patients when I was there, so the income was low and the expenses were as great as if they were filled to capacity. Anne thought the services were greatly needed and that there was more community interest than the hospital personnel were aware of.

A major player in this drama was Maggie, the cook. She was a bit of living history, a true sourdough. She seemed hesitant to talk with me at first, maybe because my somewhat formal attire contrasted with her gingham dress and white apron. However, after a few minutes of visiting, I told her about my Army experiences, and she became cordial and told me about coming to Wrangell in '98. She described how for the next fifty years she had cooked for logging camps, construction camps, and a hospital in Canada before returning to Wrangell. She looked and talked as though she had fit right in with the gold miners, and through her stories I could feel the excitement and trials of feeding those adventurers.

Maggie had been the cook in this hospital several years earlier and had worked hard to help pay off the debt they had incurred at that time. When the hospital went back into debt, the board begged her to come back. She had said that she would stay for two months, but the debt was bigger now. She talked about the amount of food needed to feed the seven people eating there daily—two patients, the doctor, two nurses, a maid, and herself. In spite of her vow to stay only two months, and even though she was lame and the work was hard, she wanted to continue to help. She confided that she was afraid the board was planning to replace her. We worked together in the kitchen several times, and before I left, I was able to tell her that the doctor had assured me that they planned to keep her if she chose to stay. Her large, somewhat toothless smile made my day.

After several meetings among all of us, the chief nurse was willing to try again to get support from the city. The Rev. Hall and the doctor asked me to study the food purchases and calculate what the prices would be if the food were purchased wholesale. My study showed that if the groceries and supplies had been bought wholesale with a cent per pound added for freight, the price per person per day would be $.58 instead of the present $.72, or a calculated yearly saving of $1,076. I cautioned that with the small census, some items should be bought locally, and so the savings might be less than that. I suggested that items such as canned fruits and vegetables should be bought in smaller cans to prevent waste. The smaller cans served six to eight, the larger ones thirty. I fulfilled the doctor's request for diet instruction sheets in order to make planning menus for patients easier. I rewrote some of the ones I had written in Petersburg. I never heard the outcome of the efforts to make changes at the hospital in Wrangell, one of the sad realities of consultant services.

Two nurses from the Ketchikan Health Department visited me at the hotel as I was recovering from a bout of what I called a twenty-four-hour flu. As with all the other community nurses I met, they had "sold" me to the local agencies even though they had no idea what this new dietary consultant was like. Was I going to act like an inspector? Would I have anything useful to offer the well-run private Catholic hospital in their city? I was becoming aware of how much of the nurses' time was taken up arranging for and teaching visitors like me when they had their own clients and community contacts to maintain.

Again, as was my experience with other nurses, we found common ground and enjoyed getting to know each other. They told me that the hospital personnel had agreed to meet with me, but the nurses sensed the food service director was reluctant to have me come. I could understand the director's reluctance, for I was finding, as Christine had so often told me, I was learning more than I was teaching. I was aware, as well, that dietitians were often considered by other medical personnel as "fuzzy-headed" and impractical, and sadly, how often the description was apt.

I was surprised when I found my suppositions were wrong in this instance. The Sister who acted as foods director merely had a case of "dietitian fear." After Sister explained that she was not a trained dietitian and had only learned how to manage from observing dietitians in other places, I assured her that on-the-job training was often the best way to learn. She showed me her beautifully run department. She was concerned about a recurring cockroach problem. I had talked with the Ketchikan sanitarian about the cockroach problem at the hospital in Wrangell. He said cockroaches came in on the produce and were difficult to control. Sister said they used spray insecticide, and she wondered about the safety of using powder under the dishwashing machine. I told her that according to the sanitarian, the way to combat cockroaches was to leave the powder for several days before removing it.

We talked a lot about Alaska, and Sister told me many things about the area that I needed to know, and her information was immensely helpful when I went to my first children's home the next day. I added her to my correspondent list, promised to send some recipes and information about foods, and enjoyed our candid talk.

The first orphanage I visited was the Guiding Light Children's Home. There were fourteen Native children, plus the son of the couple who managed the home. There was no funding organization; the husband worked outside the home. They said that their food bills were $325 a month, which included everything except a few gifts and the family's own poultry. They ordered very skillfully. We talked about dried skim milk and powdered eggs. I promised to send recipes and Extension bulletins to help with menus. The wife was bothered that the children wanted foods like fish chowder, while her husband wanted corn fritters. There was no mention of what food patterns the children had been used to and which tribal backgrounds they came from, and again, I didn't ask. I was aware how important food preferences were in all settings and so I sent recipes for both fish chowder and corn fritters. I should have realized that the children's preference for fish chowder might have come from their Native foodways.

I enjoyed the more luxurious hotel in Ketchikan and the vibrant stateside feeling of the city. With the many cruise ships and visitors, Ketchikan had frequent contact with the Lower 48. I was happy with the friends I had made in the southeast region. I decided that having met the people, correspondence might suffice for future exchanges of information, especially since Helen Amos would often be in the area.

I liked the familiar activities so much that I envied Helen's assignment as a traditional public health nutritionist in this fascinating region. I wanted to be a part of the villages I had visited. I wanted to know if the young girl cooking on the fishing boat was able to lose weight. My envy was misplaced and short-lived because I found that my own assignment not only allowed me to explore the different climates and cultures of the territory but also to be a part of the activities in many and varied communities. My next field trip to the North would convince me that I wanted to learn to like muktuk.

The hospitality of the nurses lasted to the end of my visit. As I went to the plane, they came along and introduced me to Mayor Ellis, who ran Ellis Airlines. He picked up my bags, and I told him that I thought it a real honor to have the mayor carry my luggage. He didn't charge me for excess baggage, either. After I was seated, he asked me if I would like to sit up front with him, for he was also the pilot. From that vantage point, I saw the snowcapped mountains and blue-green water that went on for miles and miles and miles all the way to Juneau.

CHAPTER 3
Anchorage, My Second Home

Fall came to Juneau, and the whole city changed. Ducks, Canada geese, and seagulls filled the sky. In 1948, we didn't have a Taku storm, but the winds blew from the sea in a chilly mist. The last salmon run of the season, the Silver, pleased bears and fishermen alike. There were fewer tourists. Government workers came to territorial offices because of their new contracts; others left having completed their one- or two-year terms. We could tell government workers from strangers, just as in Vermont we could identify summer people, or flatlanders, as we called them. Everyone started to wear warmer jackets, hats, and gloves. I was eager to go north for what was planned to be a month's field trip.

When the health department announced the hiring of a dietary consultant, the first request for services had come from Kanakanak Hospital near Dillingham in the southwest area. They asked for a remedy for flour with weevils, how to deal with smelly eggs, and help with ordering food eighteen months in advance of delivery. I thought addressing these requests sounded like fun and the solutions within my expertise, so Kanakanak was slated to be my first place to visit in the North after fulfilling some requests and teaching classes in Anchorage.

I was excited over the plan to visit what many people called the "real" Alaska, the interior, but I was also eager to see the biggest city, considered too industrialized to be part of the territory. One of my friends said, "I am so glad you are going to Anchorage, it is so easy to get to Alaska from there!"

The big plane from Juneau stopped some two hundred yards from Merrill Field terminal in Anchorage. It was a small building by airport standards in the Lower 48, but a big one compared to most terminals in Alaska. The nearly five-hour flight had gone fast, and the nine hours of October daylight faded into dusk as we landed. Several inches of snow and the plane's lights kept the airport from being completely dark. Two big governmental installations, Elmendorf Air Force Base and Fort Richardson, made this a busy airport.

Although the terrain seemed flat after the mountains of the Southeast, daylight revealed the Chugach, Kenai, and Talkeetna ranges standing a respectful distance from the city. I thought that no mountains would dare to push the largest city of the territory into the sea. The area in which we landed was called the Anchorage Bowl. Most of the white residents were as unaware as I of the Native people who had settled the Bowl and of their descendants who still lived a subsistence lifestyle there.

The airplane door opened, and I gathered my luggage and descended to the snow-packed runway. Two nurses from the Anchorage Health Department met me and took my bags. We became friends right from the start. They soon got me settled at the Anchorage Hotel and then outlined my work. The hotel was a busy place, full of white people coming and going from all parts of the territory as well as from the Lower 48. A few were dressed in business suits and conventional overcoats, but many wore parkas and waterproof boots.

The bar was full most nights, and cashiers gave silver dollars for change, even though I bought only a Coca-Cola. This silver-dollar custom intrigued a speaker at the spring ANS conference, and he insisted that I accompany him to collect silver dollars as he visited the bars on Fifth Street. He carried along a paper bag for his bounty. Many bars and very few hours of sleep did not seem to have impaired his ability to lecture the next morning. When I saw him off on a plane to Florida, he was still carrying his stockpile of heavy money in his paper bag.

The hotel, a refuge from snow and cold, became the base for all my trips in and out of Anchorage. The staff always found me a room even when I had no reservation. I didn't expect to stay in the interior for nine months, but the requests for help kept coming in. Return travel to Juneau was expensive, so I stayed.

Anchorage Daily Times, October 3, 1948, page 1. Easton Collection

The Anchorage Health Department was a busy place. Dr. O'Malley, the director, had announced my visit in the newspaper and on the radio, so there were many and varied requests waiting for me. The prevailing opinion about Native foods was expressed in a cartoon in the *Anchorage Daily Times*, October 23, 1948, with the caption: "Dietary Expert to Open Courses Here—Don't Know What All the Fuss Is About—No Matter How You Slice It—It Still Tastes Like Blubber." Never before or since was I the subject of a cartoon, much less a front-page one. Although my reports were haphazardly stored for more than sixty years in various packing cases, this now browned and ragged cartoon has always remained in my personal files.

The cartoon and announcements prompted the two radio stations, KENI and KYBR, to invite me onto their morning programs. Mrs. Walls of station KENI asked me to be on a program for women at 10:30 a.m., October 29, 1948. In an informal discussion, we talked about how to save money when buying food for a family. I recommended powdered eggs for seventy-five cents a dozen, saving three cents per egg. I suggested that husbands who had disliked Army powdered eggs might like the newer version, now commercially available and, if properly prepared, better tasting than the earlier type. I spoke about teaching children to drink reconstituted powdered milk and evaporated milk and reminded the listeners that condensed milk is mainly sugar and should be considered a dessert ingredient. Mrs. Walls offered to announce our classes and asked me to come back in January.

The audience for the programs was mainly women with small children. Many military people had decided to remain in the territory or had gone home after discharge and returned with their families, so in 1948 communities of military personnel and their families surrounded the bases. Homesteaders were also arriving. Just as the Native populations were forced to change food patterns, the new Alaskans had to make adjustments because of seasonal availability of food and limited supplies. They had problems staying within their food budgets and finding familiar store-bought foods. Isolation from families and the absence of near neighbors created problems for young parents who were homesteading and not prepared to raise children without their extended families.

The next day at station KYBR, I got the feeling that the announcer expected a dull dissertation. During station breaks he and I chatted, and after I found out that he had two children of his own, we changed the script and had a practical discussion. He asked about food likes and dislikes of children and how to handle them. We got even more response than on the previous day's program. He offered as much time as I wanted for nutrition programs in the future and even suggested that I give a whole series. After hearing from the number of people in Anchorage and Palmer who heard both broadcasts, I thought this would be a worthwhile project, but my priority was to go into remote areas to visit the hospitals and children's homes.

The radio interviews made me a sort of celebrity. I met many women who had heard both programs and found the information helpful. I was not savvy enough to take those opportunities to talk about the wealth of indigenous foods in the area or about hunting and fishing. Families who homesteaded certainly needed berries, greens, and game to survive. Reaching these women was important because they were probably hunting alongside the men.

The health department had planned for me to teach two classes, but enrollments were small despite the newspaper notices, the cartoon, the radio interviews, and an announcement of a nursery for the children. The idea of community nutrition classes was new, and perhaps the word "nutrition" was a bit frightening. The women who came were interested, though, and they immediately told their friends what they had learned. The first class had twelve people who came to every meeting and five more who came to most of them.

We decided to offer a night class for women who worked during the day. The evening class started with two young women who drove all the way from the Army post in the snow and dark, and they attended every meeting. The next session had four attendees. Among them they fed seventeen youngsters. At the third session, four jumped to ten.

Some of the women said that they had paid more attention to the feeding of their children than their own nutrition. One woman had four children under ten and had gained sixty pounds while living in Alaska. She said, "I didn't know I was so stupid. I thought if I filled the kids up, I did well." She made what I considered the most intelligent observation when asked to critique her experience: "More women should hear about the class because they won't change when they are told they are doing wrong, but if they come to a class, they don't feel anyone is talking just to them."

I probably should have called them cooking classes because I had some sort of food to prepare and taste at every session. There was great interest in the use of powdered eggs and milk, weight control, learning to shop in Alaska, bread making, and the purchase and preparation of protein foods. In one demonstration, I cooked pork liver, which most of them had never eaten although they were familiar with calf's liver. After the last class, I felt that even though the total number attending was small, I influenced the nutritional health of many children, helped the women adjust to a new lifestyle, and provided them with a social outlet.

These classes would have been a perfect place to tell newcomers about the food culture of the Native people. If I had known the community resources better, I could have obtained game from the Fish and Game Department to cook for them. I could have introduced them to salmon strips, a wonderful snack, which they could make themselves. If I had taught more about indigenous foods and the cultural sophistication of the Natives who lived from the land, I could have improved the diets of the new immigrants and their families, as well teach them to respect the Native foodways. The classes were considered a success by the health department, and there were requests for more of them.

The Extension Service at the University of Alaska had recently published several bulletins telling how Native foods could be preserved and prepared. These bulletins gave advice for hunting, an essential part of the Native foodways, developed through generations of contact with the land. Native people respected the gifts from the land and practiced good stewardship of the animal and plant resources. All parts of the animals were used either as human food, dog food, clothing, or for making tools and boats. Preparation for the hunt included care of the equipment, careful cleaning of storage areas, and spiritual preparation of the Native hunter and the hunter's family. Although I didn't learn about the spiritual components of Native foodways until my later visits, this was and still is a mark of respect for the relationship between hunter and prey.

After living in Alaska, I was never amused by the absurd expression, "As useless as selling refrigerators to Eskimos." In my first visit I found out how badly refrigeration was needed, even in the Arctic. A few of the institutions I visited had inadequate refrigerators powered by gas generators. The Native people had devised ingenious ways to keep food in cold tunnels and caches.

The need for a full-time nutritionist in Anchorage became clear to me in those early weeks. The role of the dietary consultant may not have been familiar to the public, but the desire for updated nutrition information was great. The many and various requests made it possible for me to go all over the city to see places that weren't on dietitians' usual schedules, like the jail and the Salvation Army shelter. A home economics teacher showed great interest in the classes, wrote some of the publicity, and talked about which problems she considered the most crucial. She took me to see a friend of hers and his wife. He had been put on an ulcer diet and had gained fifty pounds. No diet instructions had been given to him except that he should drink malted milk shakes. He had no idea of the calorie content of food. With five small children in the family, they were finding his suggested diet a financial strain. They were grateful for my advice about how to cut sugar and fat in the meals and curtail expenses. The consultation made being a clinical dietitian a joy.

Mrs. Powell, the chief health department sanitarian, saw how compatible our two areas of concern were. The food safety programs of the Health Department were as new as the nutrition programs. In Ketchikan I had seen how much help sanitarians and dietitians could be to each other. Anchorage sanitarians came to the nutrition classes and explained how to prevent food-borne illnesses. Many of the women were using private, untested water supplies. Most were interested in both home and restaurant sanitation. Classes ran overtime because they would not stop asking questions.

Mrs. Powell asked me to speak to the food handlers' classes to demonstrate how to prepare foods and how to set an attractive table service. She also wanted me to provide some information for them about their personal habits. The response was good; there were questions and comments from the restaurant owners about quantity food preparation. I was convinced that more work with public eating-places was needed. Many people, including me, were entirely dependent on restaurants for their food.

As a result of her good advice, I developed what appeared to be a safe way to have milk, my main beverage, with my meals. All my life I had drunk milk, and I needed its nutrients in my personal foodway. In some of my first trips to villages in southeast Alaska, I found that milk supplies were much more westernized than in the Arctic and sub-Arctic. Fresh milk was available in some southeastern towns and in Fairbanks. I drank raw milk all my youth, but here—though I hoped the Alaska cows were as carefully cared for as the six on our small Vermont farm—I didn't want to take chances. I chose to drink evaporated milk even though it was more expensive than powdered milk. I took my small can of evaporated milk and an opener that we Army people called a "church key" with me to the restaurants. On arrival, I ordered a half glass of water, added drops of chlorine, stirred the water, and let it sit until I was nearly through eating. I then added the can of milk. I learned to tolerate and almost like the mixture, but I didn't crave it when I moved away.

The requests the health department compiled for nutrition information and presentations all came from white organizations. I deemed these requests important and within the province of a public health nutritionist, if not really the core responsibilities of a dietary consultant. Girl Scout leaders wanted to have a talk for girls and their parents about nutrition and suggestions for earning a food badge. I did what they asked. Later, I had similar requests from other Girl Scout troops. I was never a Scout and thought that 4-H Clubs, more in tune with rural living, would have been more suited to Alaska, but the leaders were not interested in my suggestions.

The Anchorage City Manager asked what could be done to help the new jailer and his wife, who did the cooking and serving of food for prisoners. I visited the jail and found good food even though the budget was limited. I suggested foods for a minimally adequate diet so they would not be criticized for pampering the inmates. Dr. O'Malley asked me to advise the jailer concerning his mild case of diabetes. The Rev. Hugh Rounds met me while I was at the jail and asked me to see the set-up at the Anchorage Mission home. The food served at the mission was low in vitamin C. The cook was planning to leave, so I wrote plans for the reverend to use until he could find another cook.

Dr. O'Malley requested that I go to the Salvation Army shelter because they were feeding fifty men every day. The food program was started in order to remove hotplates from the sleeping quarters. The meals were entirely the men's responsibilities, and there had been quarrels over their contributions to the food kitty. The manager's wife had taken over the arduous job of keeping track of the money and was sorry she had taken it on. I could sympathize with the amount of work the accounting took. I visited the shelter twice, and in the week between our meetings, I saw a long article in the *Forty-Ninth Star* about the program. When we got together the second time, I congratulated her for keeping the men out of the hospitals. She decided doing the bookkeeping wasn't such an imposition after all.

During two visits to Valley Hospital I was able to help the substitute cook with some recipes and suggestions on how to utilize the inconvenient kitchen and storage space. The doctors were interested in a diet manual, especially in diets for prenatal and post-partum cases. One of the public health nurses asked me to teach nutrition to her New Mothers' Class. Most of the women were almost ready to deliver, so we spent little time on pregnancy diets and more on general nutrition, nursing diets, and child feeding. I should have made more inquiries about what they had already been told. After I explained the advantages of breastfeeding, some of the women said their doctor didn't approve of breastfeeding. I explained that as a dietitian, I thought the nutritional advantages for the baby were great, but, of course, the doctor might have good reasons for his advice, and they should follow it.

The community health nurses took me to three children's homes in which many of the children were Native. They took me along as an expert, but I think I did more learning than teaching. Christine Heller had visited the same homes a year earlier and taught the managers and cooks about indigenous foods they could make good use of. They were eager for me to tell Miss Heller that they now put up rosehips.

The Cather Home had sixteen children and fed them with produce from its own farm. The manager asked about freezing rosehip pulp and salmon eggs. She had feeding problems. Her twelve-year-old daughter had a bad skin condition, and Billy, a four-year-old, refused to eat solid food. She had not considered the possibility that Billy might have sore gums. We suggested not making him eat if he didn't want to. The nurse said she would keep an eye on Billy and see how this strategy worked.

The Davis Home had sixteen children, five of whom were very young. Two of them were from a set of triplets. Now two years old, they still did not walk or talk. After accompanying the nurses on these visits, I was reminded of the importance of community health nurses in nutrition education. I still remember those two-year-olds.

At the Valley Christian Home for children, I joined a health department team to observe the BCG (a skin test for tuberculosis) technique. Although the tuberculosis epidemic was abating, it was

Small children's home 1949. Easton Collection.

still a major scourge that would continue for a long time. The rate of incidence as late as 1966 was still ten times the national average, and the infant mortality rate was among the highest in the world. When Alaska achieved statehood, the life expectancy of a Native was 34.7 years, while a white Alaskan could expect to live for seventy years.

The health department personnel working with the schools received many requests for me to speak to public school classes about nutrition. In classes at the University of Michigan, the professor of health education taught that no one should ever use precious time teaching in the schools, giving the teachers a rest. She said we should work with the teachers so that our information would fit into the curriculum and be an integral part of the whole learning process. She would not have approved of many of my activities at the schools. I did not find these requests a waste of time, although I understood that my main duty was to help communities and institutions. I remembered that when we had visitors at my tiny high school of one hundred students in Vermont, I learned a great deal, even if their topics didn't fit the curriculum.

Many educators at the time advocated that the best way to teach adults was to teach the children first. I didn't approve of telling children to go home and teach their families; this idea was in conflict with the Native tenet that wisdom came to the children from their Elders. As a public health nutritionist, especially in areas where a variety of food cultures existed, I wanted the parents to hear the information first and consider how it fit into their lives.

One high school home economics teacher asked me to talk to her girls about what nutritionists and dietitians did and what training they needed. She had noticed that the youngsters had little chance to learn about the vocational fields open to them. The talk was timed to last fifteen minutes, but the students were so interested the discussion lasted the whole hour.

The request, almost a command, to visit the Anchorage school lunch program was in answer to complaints made to the Anchorage Department of Health from the community. The leaders sent me a list of questions about conditions in the lunchroom that discouraged students from eating there. Federally supported school lunch programs were relatively new in Alaska. I discovered these programs were a part of my workload whether I wanted them to be or not. I met with the superintendent, school lunch manager, and principal, all of whom appeared to be willing to cooperate to make changes. I talked to the PTA, an active group of about two hundred people, a third of them fathers. I pointed out that the high school had an open campus at noon, and the older students went to stores or restaurants nearby. Some of the younger groups came to school in shifts, thereby eating all their meals at home. Many did not eat at all and roamed around the city during the lunch period, and some of them bought orange drink rather than milk, which was the same price.

An official inspection was required. I disliked being an inspector because it made me appear to be an enemy instead of a source of help. I toured the facility and then discussed my findings with everyone. I did not have the time to address these problems because that would have required full-time supervision. I sent an official report to the Juneau office, stating that the meals served met the required patterns, but participation was too low. I never knew whether this report was read and assumed it was not.

Even though the program was under new management the next year and the quality of the food had improved, there was no change in participation. Of the twenty-seven hundred students enrolled, only two hundred children ate lunch. A participation rate of 7 percent was woefully low. The PTA and the administrators appeared to find me more of a nuisance than a help; I was not the savior they wanted.

My other school lunch activities in the areas were a lot more fun. At Palmer, where I visited several times, the whole scene was different. Once I borrowed a small pickup truck from the health department motor pool. I set off on icy roads to drive the twelve miles to see how the school lunch program was doing. The road was narrow between huge snowdrifts. Suddenly I was pointed back toward Anchorage with the nose of the truck nuzzled in a snow bank, headed the opposite direction of where I wanted to go. I got out of the cab and looked hopelessly at my vehicle. A car came along, and who should it be but the manager of the Anchorage Hotel who had seen me leave that morning. After teasing me about not knowing which direction I was going, he shoveled some snow into the open bed of the truck, backed it out and headed me toward Palmer. He said he would have a few choice words for the carpool manager who let me get on the road without any ballast.

I enjoyed telling the superintendent and the manager at Palmer how well I thought they were doing in the face of several obstacles. The children who brought their lunches did not make good choices. Some brought milk from home, some bought it at school, but many had none at all, and several vowed they never drank milk. One group ate only ice cream. The superintendent was aware of the situation and said that they were working on it with the parents and teachers. We talked about some cost-cutting measures in the hope that they could break even financially.

Another school lunch program that was even more surprising, and for which I could take no credit, was in the tiny town of Wasilla. In my early days in Anchorage, I had some talks with Wasilla school personnel. They really wanted to have a school lunch program, but the health department advisors, which in this case included me, could see no way that they could find suitable space for one. The only possible room was an attic with no stairs.

None of us envisioned that I would submit an official administrative report two years later that included, "No routine yes and no

answers can adequately tell the story of the Wasilla lunch program."
In an attic formerly available only by ladder, the teachers and townspeople built a stairway to an attractive school lunch kitchen and
dining room. On a stormy day the nurse and I visited this charming
facility. Only 22 of the 125 students were present because of the
weather. Usually 90 children, a participation rate of 72 percent, ate
in the dining room. The nurse said that she had noticed a definite
improvement in the physical conditions of the children.

Everyone at the health department in Anchorage helped me
prepare my field kit because they knew what I would need for the
upcoming visit to the Southwest. They procured a secondhand 16-
mm movie camera and a Kodak to take slides. I was never techni-
cally proficient with camera equipment and learned only the bare
essentials of photography. I didn't know which f-stops to use, even
though I attended a lot of evening get-togethers where the hosts
showed slides and carefully detailed the distances, lenses, and techniques they had used. Those sessions were the principal form of
entertainment all over the territory.

Colleagues also helped me with my wardrobe because I needed
clothes for going into the field. These would be "cold weather"
clothes, different than I had ever owned. When I went to the University of Vermont, we were not allowed to wear slacks to class.
If the weather approached zero, we could wear ski pants for the
half-mile walk between buildings but had to take them off before
going into the classroom. In Ann Arbor, I had worn parts of my gray,
commonly called "pink," Army uniforms that had been altered and
dyed black for civilian practicality. My friends knew people all over
Anchorage. They found me the second-hand tan twill parka with
the fur-lined hood and quilted red lining that I wore the rest of my
stay.

I dreaded leaving my Anchorage Hotel refuge, but the Kanakanak
Hospital's pesky weevils and smelly eggs had been on my to-do list
for a long time. Dr. O'Malley and his department were pleased with
what I had done and the interest in nutrition I had generated in the
area. They wanted me to schedule return visits, but I knew that the
remote hospitals and orphanages were my main focus. I was ready
to go southwest into the rural areas.

I found a bush pilot and made a reservation to fly to Dillingham, subject to lots of conditions based on the weather. The small planes that had floats in the summer became ski planes with the snow. I was anxious, at last, to see some of what people called "the real Alaska," weather permitting.

CHAPTER 4

The Real Alaska, Kanakanak and Dillingham

"You had better pick out a good spot." The pilot's voice was suddenly loud, for the noise in the cockpit had gone silent, the engine dead. "If I can't start the engine, we have to land." The beautiful, almost-snow-covered peaks did not look so beautiful at that moment.

"Everything looks pretty soft from here," I said calmly. The engine sputtered, the plane shook a bit, and we continued our flight toward the western coast.

The pilot might have been testing me to see if I would fit into the Alaskan scene. I am sure he reported to others, especially the radio operators, that I wasn't frightened. All the young men in the field took the vetting of newly arrived female medical personnel, usually nurses, very seriously. Later I checked my suspicion with my brother Frank, who had taken me for my first plane ride, also in a Piper Cub. He verified that a clever pilot could stop and start his plane in midair.

At about ten o'clock, first light in those November days, I had boarded the Piper Cub, owned and flown by Dennis, a handsome bush pilot. Once in the air, he pointed out important spots in the snow-covered terrain below. He showed me where a pilot had recently had a fatal crash. When he told me that the man was named Ted, with an unpronounceable last name, I knew whom he was talking about. During Prohibition, Ted had made frequent trips to and from northern Vermont into Canada. Though I was too young to know about the illegal nature of his cargo, I knew federal authorities had tried to catch him after he crashed his plane near my home. When Dennis suggested I look for a landing place, I was musing about how Ted had managed to get from the Vermont woods to Alaska without his plane or anyone in our town ever hearing of his escape. I could now write the people at home that Ted met his fate in Alaskan mountains.

After the suggestion we might crash, my first ride with a real Alaska bush pilot ended uneventfully. Upon arrival at Dillingham, men and boys, young and old, greeted us, running through the snow blown up by the plane's skis. Winds blew the cargo out of the hands of the men unloading the plane, and bags went scooting across the ice. I could see my trusty Valpak, typewriter, and other gear being rescued by young boys. So I would not also scoot across the snow, strong arms grabbed me as I emerged, far from gracefully. Other volunteers held down the plane. Women, many with small children peeking out of their parkas, and girls stood apart from the plane to watch. Most of them wore bright cloth covers over their parkas because the warmest way to wear a parka was with fur against the body. They made bright spots in the snow. A similar ceremony occurred for every plane that came in. The townspeople also waved away departing passengers. The children were not there if school was in session, but they were well aware which planes had come or gone.

Dennis was my pilot for several flights. With his blond hair and blue eyes, he looked as though he was of Norwegian blood, perhaps from Petersburg in the Southeast. I came to know his equally attractive wife and three little girls, all with the same blond, blued-eyed look. Several nights I slept on their couch waiting for the weather to clear for our flight. His wife was gracious when I failed to correctly remember a recipe for chocolate cake. I felt guilty about wasting her precious commodities on the too-liquid batter. She said it was worth it not to dread entertaining a dietitian again. I was photographed shoveling out the outhouse next to their home after a big storm. Someone had left the door open, and it took a great deal of shoveling to make the outhouse useful again.

I don't know why I wasn't afraid on flights around Alaska. It may be that I felt safe on my first plane ride from a Craftsbury meadow in March 1941, when my brother took me up. After that, I was a passenger in all sorts of planes flown by daring pilots while in India and at Maxwell Field, Alabama. Big planes to me always were and still are a means to get to places quickly, but small planes are part of the earth and sky.

Women and girls watch arrival of plane, 1948. Easton Collection

I had heard that a Russian-Eskimo Elder said when she was told a dietary consultant was coming, "Tell her we eat what we have. If she wants to help, bring a bomber with food." Throughout my journey I wished many times I had access to that bomber and never more than this first time I went southwest of Anchorage.

The Bristol Bay area and part of the Aleutian Chain were served by the ANS Hospital at Kanakanak, one of the bigger rural hospitals and isolated from the nearest village, Dillingham. The language and food habits of the Eskimo, Aleut, Athabascan Indian, Filipino, and white people were all found there. Since there were no roads connecting to the mainland, all patients had to come by ship or air to Dillingham and be met by a hospital vehicle.

The hospital's chief engineer put my luggage in a truck and took me over rutted and treacherous roads to the hospital, six miles south of Dillingham, for what I thought was a routine visit, requested months ago. My schedule had been planned so that I could go to Kanakanak Hospital to help with weevils, smelly eggs, and the orders for food that would come in on a barge eighteen months in the future. Immediately the doctor and chief nurse told me they had a food shortage that was at a crisis level. This was no routine visit.

Dr. John Libby had come to the hospital earlier that year after there had been no physician for several years. He and Miss Betty Riley, the recently arrived chief nurse, told me how worried they were about the low level of existing supplies and the poor morale of the employees. I could not believe that their gloomy outlook was well founded until we made a food inventory on my first day. Betty and I counted the existing foods almost all that night. In trying to estimate the exact amount of food available, my military experience in small hospitals was invaluable. I knew the number of servings in each size can, could estimate census changes, and was good at simple mathematics even without an adding machine. There was no such thing as a handheld calculator. Together we figured out what food was on hand and made the unpleasant conclusion: there was far too little food for the immediate future. Betty had a wonderful sense of humor, and we worked well together. As each startling fact emerged, we came up with impossible but funny solutions.

At all ANS hospitals in the northern areas, food deliveries came on barges in the summer when the ice was out. Orders had to be placed eighteen months in advance, and someone, usually the head nurse, had to figure out what the hospital would need for delivery in two years and choose the appropriate items from an ANS catalogue. To complicate matters at this hospital, the time to prepare that food order coincided with the current food shortage, so the order had to wait.

Their next shipment, which had been ordered by Betty's predecessor, also a nurse without food service experience, was not expected to arrive by barge for at least ten months. Shipments of emergency rations could be flown in, but at exorbitant prices. These shortages occurred because the orders for food that had been made two years earlier were too small and the most popular foods had been eaten first. Dr. Libby had already notified the Juneau office but had had no reply. He appreciated my offer to write to them with more specific, disturbing details. Neither of our appeals brought the needed food for months.

As a dietitian, one of the worst things I found was that all of the peanut butter, usually a great emergency source of protein, was rancid. There was bad news about other protein foods: a week's worth of eggs, enough fish for 18 days, and a 30-day supply of meat. Those shortages were topped by the fact that the only canned vegetables remaining were nineteen cases of spinach and corn, those least liked by everyone. All the best-liked fruit was gone too, leaving a 204-day supply of canned peach halves, the slippery kind in thick, sugary syrup. It was no wonder that the people were unhappy with the monotony of the food. The 630-day supply of butter had been a major ordering error and would probably become rancid soon. Betty and I found that our funny comments during the inventory turned to gallows humor.

Two of the original requests for my help were easily dispatched. The flour has weevils. Easy, sift the little black critters out, but don't worry if you don't get them all. The baking process will sanitize the flour. Except for possible cosmetic concerns, the bread will be wholesome. However, if there are lots of weevils, the flour will be spoiled and should be destroyed. I never dared suggest that the weevils would contribute small amounts of protein.

The eggs smelled too strong. Just keep them as cool as possible but not at freezing temperature. Turn them over every two weeks and realize that the sulfur compounds formed are not offensive to people who have lived with strong eggs for years. In fact, when people who were used to the strong eggs went to the Lower 48, they found fresh eggs tasteless.

Miss Conner, the cook, and two helpers prepared three meals a day for fifty people: thirteen women, seven men, and ten children who were patients, and twenty employees. The patients were Natives as were some attendants, but no allowance was made for their food preferences. Some of the professionals at the hospital were from the large, prestigious Loma Linda Hospital in California and endorsed vegetarian diets, with no stimulants such as coffee, tea, or chocolate. Alaska was not a good place for non-meat eaters at the best of times and certainly not in the present food crisis. I was told several times that missionaries who promoted a vegetarian diet told Native people that their ancestors had sinned by eating meat.

Betty was a creative, cheerful person, and we set about finding ways to improve the crisis situation. We thought through possible so-

lutions with Miss Conner, who was cooperative and innovative. She
was a fine manager with a great sense of humor. The variety of food
was dismal, but together we came up with ideas, some ridiculous,
but some that helped make effective changes. I remembered our
food shortages during the Depression in Vermont, and later while
in the military, the terrible supplies I was issued to feed hospital-
ized service men and employees in Karachi. My staff of soldiers had
enjoyed decorating for Christmas, so I suggested we might try some
cosmetic things to celebrate Thanksgiving. No plans had been made
for making the menus different from ordinary days, and with the
help of one of the nurses, the cook, and Betty, I scrambled around.
We made nut cups from yellow onionskin typing paper and used the
orange sheets from the x-ray packages for tray covers. We filled the
cups with candy made from lumpy brown sugar.

The medical staff's table had nut cups and centerpieces with
candles, boughs, and a few fresh oranges. The attendants, who were
local, had not set their table. The Native people had no Thanksgiving
traditions and little for which to be thankful. A nurse suggested that
there was no point in making a centerpiece for them. I did not know
whether this advice was a form of discrimination toward Native
people or just an acknowledgment of the hospital's custom of seating
the medical staff at a separate table. I made a festive centerpiece for
the attendants' table anyway and was pleased to have several of the
girls thank me for doing it. The decorations did create some pleasure
in the meal, but I knew that Thanksgiving frills were not a solution
to the food problems.

We made out menus for six weeks to prorate the food so that it
would be used as wisely as possible. I found some cases of sweetened
condensed milk in the almost empty meat freezer. We made this into
freezer ice cream. We had rescued a large amount of flour from the
weevils, and there was nearly a two-month supply of sugar; that
meant we could bake more often. We froze some freshly baked rolls
to reheat and have hot bread, making the meals slightly more ap-
petizing.

One day Miss Conner made some wonderful dark bread, a treat
for the staff. She had found some molasses and mixed it with ground
oatmeal. One of the nurses told her that the bread was good, but it

looked as though it had been made with whole-wheat flour, and she didn't think there was any. Miss Conner replied, "No, I didn't use whole wheat flour. You know our mixer is broken, so I mixed it with my feet." The nurse laughed and hurried off to share the joke.

I was sorry that I didn't have more contact with the patients themselves. There was, I understood, a great deal of dissatisfaction among them about the food, and I didn't wonder. I spent some time in the children's wards, but had very little contact with the other patients. Betty said there would be little I could do about their complaints anyway. I realized later that I could have learned more about the foods that were familiar to them, ones they liked. I could also have given them some advice for when they returned to their families.

Dr. Libby asked me to make out several diet sheets for him. I readapted the Petersburg diets, leaving out the fresh fruits and vegetables and adding the diets he needed. I also instructed an outpatient for him. The need for a territorial diet manual was reinforced. My visit was well timed for me to learn about crises that could come up in remote areas, but ill timed as far as the morale of the hospital personnel was concerned. I learned just before I left that none of the staff realized that my visit was supposed to be a routine one. They thought that I had come to solve the food-shortage problem.

The staff asked that I tell them what I had done. At a meeting on the last day I was there, I told them that we had made an inventory and reported it to Dr. Googe, the director of ANS Hospitals in Juneau; that Dr. Libby was going to see that there would be more and better food supplies; what a good cook Miss Conner was and how well she was doing under the circumstances; that they were being very helpful about the situation, for it certainly was not interesting to be living on canned corn, spinach and slippery peach halves; that I thoroughly enjoyed working with them and appreciated their cooperation, though not every person did cooperate.

Nurses asked whose fault it was. I tried to make it clear that I didn't feel it was anyone's fault. The personnel who had done the ordering were new at the time, and all of them had since left, so they hadn't had time to benefit from their experience. I told them that Miss Conner and I were working on a guide to help with the new order, now due.

Amazingly enough, this presentation of "what I didn't do" seemed to have a good effect. One of the nurses remarked that she was glad to know that something was being done, for she had felt that no one cared. Another one told me that they had been afraid that I was going to say that they should have been using what they had more wisely or make some outlandish suggestions for menus. Dietitians were sometimes thought to have weird ideas, and I was glad they didn't consider me as one of those. Ordering food was a challenge for all the hospitals, but I never found as severe a food shortage as I did at Kanakanak.

The problems of working in isolated areas were common to most of the hospitals and children's homes. The homes were generally church sponsored, and the staffs were missionaries, many of them trained for fieldwork. They knew how badly they were needed and worked long hours. In visits to several institutions, I was aware of the Herculean efforts the workers put into trying to feed, teach, and care for the children in a land so inhospitable, especially in the winter.

In some ways I think the staffs of the hospitals had a more difficult time adjusting to the intense cold, the dark, and isolation than the staffs of the children's homes. The hospital workers were trained at medical centers in the Lower 48. They were unused to working twenty-four hours a day, seven days a week and living in isolated buildings far from even a small village. I suspected that some women had been recruited or at least influenced by news articles like the one written by Richard Neuberger in the *New York Times Magazine,* March 6, 1949, titled, "It's a Woman's World Anyway in Alaska," subtitled, "Unwed Girls Are as Rare as Amicable Bears, so the Men Dance as the Ladies Call the Tunes." There were places in Alaska where some of us lucky ones had a great social life, but most of the ANS hospitals were not in those places. I was sure that the Kanakanak nurses had not been aware of the isolation, the darkness, and lack of organized entertainment when they signed on. The situation contributed to the low morale among medical personnel and was exacerbated at Kanakanak by the terrible food.

I returned to Dillingham four months later and got to visit with Betty again. She was still working to improve the hospital food situation although a lot of the "we can't do it" attitude had persisted, even with the new supplies. Some personnel were leaving because they were dissatisfied, others were completing their contracts, and newly hired staff would be coming soon. Some loyal staff stayed, sure that the next year would be better. Dorothy Root, the community nurse in Dillingham and Betty's good friend, wrote me several years later that she was the bridesmaid at the wedding of Betty and the hospital maintenance engineer. The whole village attended and cheered.

The Alaska Crippled Children's Association helped me with the community events because Miss Dorothy Root had gone for a brief vacation in the states. The women in the association helped me notify potential class members and advised me about how to tailor the classes. My time in Dillingham gave me the experience I wanted in an established community where all the citizens were concerned with common problems.

The foodways of Dillingham changed rapidly after the end of the Second World War and with the increased commercialization of fishing. Although there were still vast indigenous resources, many Native people worked on fishing boats or in the canneries. They did not harvest and store sufficient food in the traditional ways. Instead of using the summer months to prepare for the winter, young adults worked for cash wages. Cash was needed to pay for utilities, for ready-made clothing, and food to replace or supplement harvested meats, fish, and greens. This money was then used to buy food for the winter: the grubstake.

Food choices made during the transition between living off the land and settling in established communities were complicated for people who were used to traditional foods and unfamiliar with store-bought foods. They may have never eaten canned fruits and vegetables and did not know that canned tomatoes were nutritionally a good replacement for greens or berries.

We decided to have the community classes patterned after the ones in Anchorage and wanted to hold them at night in one of the village school's classrooms. While I was arranging for the classes, the principal, Mr. George Linn, asked if I would be willing to talk to the students. I agreed that on the days that I held adult classes, I would talk to the schoolchildren in their classrooms. Use of the school building outweighed any reluctance I had for teaching in regular grade school classes. My Michigan professor, who advised against such activities, never worked in the Alaskan bush, or she would have realized that one needed to be flexible enough to barter teaching time for classroom space.

We gave a three-week nutrition unit in the school in tandem with the community classes for adults. The teachers and I were amazed that the children wanted to talk about food instead of having recess. Three groups of classes were chosen: a high school group, seventh and eight grades, and the fourth, fifth, and sixth grades. I found that the youngsters not only listened to what I said, but went home, started drinking milk, and brought their mothers to the community classes at night.

I taught the lower grades about the "Wheel of Good Eating," a commercial poster that illustrated the recommended USDA pattern for food intake. I showed them that they could get everything on it in Dillingham. They had a great time talking about the foods growing around them, and we compiled a list of berries and greens that they would look for in the summer. They made copies of it for their classrooms and gave me one. They had included dandelion greens, berries, and powdered milk on it. I was finally talking to both adults and children, Native and White together, about the food wealth of the land. I was witnessing a historical change in food cultures.

The high school had a more detailed course, linked to biology classes. Since many of the pupils were old for their grades, we had a discussion about weight gain and loss, as well as the nutritional requirements of adolescence. They took a great interest and bombarded me with questions as to what foods one should take on a trap line and what did Alaska foods have in them. My memories of my brothers' trap lines, although much smaller and less vital to the family table or purse, helped me make my information pertinent. One of the boys asked if I thought sweetened condensed milk, Eagle Brand, was a good thing to take. This gave me a chance to tell them that condensed milk was mostly sugar and wasn't good to feed children and babies, but was great to take on a trap line to sweeten beverages such as coffee and tea because it didn't freeze.

All the groups kept diet records, which they evaluated themselves. I found that the high schoolers drank the least milk; most of the children drank great quantities of pop, expensive at 20 cents a bottle, ate candy, and chewed bubble gum. A common lunch was two dishes of ice cream. Many ate no breakfast, but the really big omission was sources of vitamin C. The students had questions about the composition of powdered and evaporated milk. Cream was mentioned during the discussion. One of the fourth graders raised his hand and asked, "What is it? Is it that yellow stuff I saw on a bottle of milk that came from Anchorage once?"

Again, my Michigan professor would have been shocked when I arrived one day to find the five younger grades all in one room. It was obvious that Mr. Linn had an administrative crisis of some sort, but I knew school protocol well enough not to inquire exactly what the problem was. He asked if I would talk to the group about something related to health to keep them quiet. We started with a discussion of health departments, which soon grew to include the Alaska Native Service and the Extension Service. When I asked if anyone knew what a "sanitarian" was, one boy said loudly, "Yes, that's a place where you bury dead people."

During this discussion, a pupil asked: "Do the people out at the hospital get the right food?" The question was evidence of the low morale of the patients and the unsuitability of the food served to them; it was evidence of a cultural clash, with the Native food-ways losing. I explained that they had very little food on hand at Kanakanak Hospital, but if the patient ate everything that was served him, he would probably get his nutritional requirements of the day. From that grew a discussion of why people like certain foods, how to learn to like new foods, and the balanced diets of different groups, including the Eskimo. I never asked Mr. Linn what the crisis was but enjoyed his expression of appreciation for my help.

I enjoyed working with the adult group. The principal's wife mentioned that she had never seen many of the women at community doings. At first I was disturbed to see five or ten little boys, fourth and fifth graders, as well as their baby siblings in the room with the village women. The boys listened eagerly, didn't squirm, were tickled to pieces if I let them stir the food I was demonstrating. I thought this juvenile attendance would decrease when they learned that they only got a taste of the things that we made, but it never did.

Author shovels path to outhouse, 1948. Easton Collection

At first the Native women didn't ask questions or make many remarks. I worried about whether they were getting the information they wanted, but they came through wind and snow to every meeting. By the last weeks, they had warmed up and thoroughly enjoyed the antics of Mrs. Stocky and Mrs. Lanky, characters in the lesson on being overweight and underweight that developed into a tale about next-door neighbors, what they do and what they eat. At the bread demonstration, I was making sweet rolls, and one lady said, "Poor Mrs. Stocky. Could she eat any of these?" By including weight control information, I reflected my personal foodway. Some of the white women wanted to control or lose weight, but the Native women were not heavy, even though their full faces and heavy clothing led people to believe they were. Perhaps the class was useful to the Native women as their lifestyles changed and they became less active, as well as helped them understand their teenaged daughters, who were already catching the "be thinner" bug.

The women were interested in the lesson about purchasing food for long periods of time and about what the schoolchildren were learning and what they ate. Most of them had two or three children in the school as well as several at home. We talked about the value of

Native game and fish, berries, and greens and started swapping ideas. The doctor's wife attended every meeting and delighted the group with this question: "What do you do to make dried apple pie? I just put the apples in the crust and they were horrible." She enjoyed the laughter as much as the rest of the class and vowed to reconstitute her dried fruit after that.

I was thoroughly convinced that demonstrations were a must. I prepared food at every meeting, although the dish had to be simple such as powdered milk cooked in cereal with dried fruit and some milk drinks. With some donations from the village women, we were able to sample string bean and raw carrot salads. We planned a meal for Mrs. Stocky and Mrs. Lanky to eat together. We cooked pork liver and powdered eggs and demonstrated bread making. Class members took down addresses to send for Extension material and recipes.

I witnessed the great desire Native mothers had for their children to succeed and be equipped to meet the challenges of new lifestyles in the larger villages. One mother approached one of the schoolteachers who also attended the community lessons. This teacher was trusted and much loved by the children. The mother asked, "Please, can you tell me about these 'lapkins' I am hearing about?" The teacher was puzzled. The mother continued, "Lapkins, yes lapkins, my children say they need them."

The teacher smiled, "Oh, you mean 'napkins.' They are little pieces of cloth or paper to wipe your fingers on after eating food so your clothes stay clean."

The mother beamed and said, "Thank you. Yes, my children will have lapkins." As I compared these Dillingham classes to the ones in Anchorage, I realized I was learning a great deal about the differences in white and Native foodways. I saw the quiet surrender of Native traditions when foodways clashed. I was sad, and yet I knew it was inevitable and hoped that the children could still appreciate their own food culture.

Again a Girl Scout leader asked me to help the girls work for a badge, this time a hostess badge. I had less enthusiasm for this group because working with the Native people fascinated me more. I had two sessions with the Scouts because the leaders were trying to help the girls be proud of the things Alaska had to offer and yet be able to feel at ease when they went to another lifestyle. Some intended to go to college, others to nurses' training. They were going to live in two worlds. I hoped that the rich Native culture would not lose out completely.

One of the most pleasing things about working in the Kanakanak/ Dillingham area was the interest in nutrition classes. There were few community activities or professional visitors in the winter. The classes fulfilled a need for the people there to know they had not been ignored since so many health services, such as mass x-rays had been promised to them, and none had made it to town. I hoped some of the interest was a result of my concern with retaining the rich foodways of the area. I realized that I was lucky Christine Heller had planned my activities in the bush for winter months when the industries were closed down. It took time to learn about the villages and the people, and I thought that a one-day or several-days visit, especially in summer months, could be far worse than none at all.

As I approached my departure, I couldn't believe I had ever wanted to have the traditional public health nutritionist's job. I wouldn't have wanted to give up working through a major food crisis and helping, at least a little. How could I have considered foregoing Mrs. Connor's pseudo whole wheat bread or talking about trap lines? I wouldn't have missed watching young boys carry their baby siblings, all in parkas, into the adult classes. Neither would I have given up laughing and almost crying with Betty nor visiting with family groups who entertained me with evenings of slide shows in impromptu gatherings.

After a wonderful party the last night I was supposed to be there, I spent two additional nights waiting for the weather to clear enough to take off. Since my friends had parties those nights as well, the stock of bathtub gin must have been depleted because they wrote that they finally had a "Thank God She's Gone" party after Dennis and I departed.

My horizons had been widened. The snow-covered peaks seemed friendlier. I knew many of the men and boys who loaded the plane and the mothers and girls who watched. Although I could say I had been to another part of the real Alaska, I was beginning to realize how different each part was and I wanted to see them all. I still hadn't learned to like muktuk.

CHAPTER 5
Kodiak, The Close of 1948

Sky and water created the backdrop for the busy seaport of Kodiak, full of fishing boats. Rocks dusted with snow plunged into the water. Large numbers of military personnel were stationed there during World War II, and the military presence continued. Vestiges of the long association with the Russians were evident in the slant and shape of rooflines. I have always remembered it as a special spot with glorious weather, cool but not cold.

Kodiak Island was a part of the real Alaska, but a distinctly different one, representing the earliest white settlements and explorations. There were about one thousand residents in Kodiak itself. We called the Native people Aleut, but actually they were Alutiiq, and experts in hunting land animals and fishing for sea mammals. The bear population reduced the herds of land mammals that were sources of food and limited the supply of small fish.

The early Russian explorers introduced wheat flour and yeast, which resulted in bread making, and tea. In the 1800s, expansion of the whaling industry along the Arctic and Pacific Oceans and the Bering Sea transformed small villages into ports with canneries and whale oil rendering plants. In southwestern Alaska, Asian workers in these commercial ventures started small patches of rice in the tidal bays. Today, Elders of the region consider rice and soy sauce as traditional foods. They continue to gather rice that was planted along marshy rivers in family fishing grounds over one hundred years before.

I did not observe the large amount of rice in the diets of the Native people on my trip to the Southwest but found, on later trips, that rice was the most common starch food because it could be stored almost indefinitely, unlike potatoes. I should have considered increasing the amount of rice in barge orders for the northern areas because even though potatoes furnished more nutrients than rice, they did not store well. In November the twenty-five hundred pounds of potatoes at Kanakanak were beginning to spoil.

Missionaries administered non-government hospitals all over Alaska. Griffin Memorial, a small Catholic hospital, served the Kodiak area and was exceptionally well run. It was adequately funded but concerned with food costs, as were all hospitals in the territory. Tuberculosis patients were sent to government hospitals on the mainland.

I had been told that in some institutions, a visiting health department person was considered an inspector or, at best, a meddling nuisance, but the Grey Nuns of the Sacred Heart showed no evidence of feeling that way. The Sister who served as the cook prepared and presented food with more artistry than any other hospital cook that I saw. Another Sister skillfully ordered the food. The kitchen was immaculate and well equipped. They had ordered a new freezer, had new electric stoves and a walk-in refrigerator. When I found there was nothing I could teach, we swapped recipes. I learned how well a twenty-person food unit could be run.

This trip was still part of my orientation and provided me with more good ideas to share with members of my growing list of correspondents. Some of my recent experiences were useful, and so I was not a complete novice. I gave out some recipes that I carried with me and added new names to my list. Besides deciphering and typing my long field reports and sending letters to involved agencies, Mary Davis, our unit secretary in Juneau, maintained what was becoming a clearinghouse of tips and recipes from each place I went. She also gathered addresses for nutrition materials and health department literature.

Since I arrived in Kodiak later in the year than I had expected to, I was fortunate that no community classes had been scheduled. Plans for celebrating Christmas were everywhere. The Island's long relationship with the Russian Orthodox Church and Catholic and Protestant missionaries meant that Christmas was an important festival. I joined the familiar cookie making and decorating at the orphanages, a welcome relief from food crises.

Miss Marion Curtis, the chief public health nurse, was an important presence in the city and a shining example of what a great community nurse could be. She had fostered an ideal relationship between the health department and the community. She established an excellent prenatal and well-baby program. Her department attended to women throughout pregnancy, visited them in the hospital, and then followed new mothers and babies at home. Marion was a wonderful hostess and later, a good correspondent. She took me on long walks in the woods to look for local plants. To my great relief, we didn't meet any bears. Years after I left Alaska, Marion wrote that she and the city had changed. "The Navy still does a lot of training here. They call it maneuvers, but they look more like 'boyeuvers' to me."

The physicians at the hospital asked me to prepare some outpatient diet sheets. Again I was reminded of the need for an Alaskan diet manual and nutrition materials that would include the indigenous food resources of the Kodiak area. The new mothers in Marion's program questioned why they weren't allowed fresh fruits and chocolate. There was also a standing order at the hospital that the new mother did not get any meat for the first three days, although she could have eggs. I asked the doctor why this was, and he said that he didn't know the directive existed. An officially adopted diet manual would have solved this kind of problem.

On a day's visit to the Kodiak Baptist Mission, I found that the staff took real interest in the children and their foodways. The superintendent had called a meeting so the staff could meet me, and we talked about food costs, menus, indigenous foods and Native food habits, school lunches, and how those issues affected the needs of the children. During the conversation, a staff person mentioned that some of the teenage girls who were overweight refused to drink milk. The women felt that the best way to reach the girls was through lessons in their classes and requested that I talk to the home economics students.

On a tour of the home, I saw the freezer and the well-organized storerooms. We discussed the use of powdered skim milk, MPF, and rosehips. The different cottages did not serve the same menus, but they all served family style and kept costs nearly identical. The mission was not luxurious, but well run with a homelike atmosphere.

Many of the adults, hardworking and with little rest, had colds, and some children had mumps. Because of these infectious conditions, I asked if dishwashing procedures were part of the problem. I saw a real need for improved dishwashing methods in all the institutions I visited and most of the children's homes in the territory. The shortage of water was a universal problem.

Impressed as I was with the Kodiak Mission, I was even more impressed with Baker Cottage in Ouzinkie, twelve miles from Kodiak City. I would not have believed that a children's home could provide such a family-like environment. The director was the main reason. I marveled at her firm, gentle handling of each child. Upon hearing that I did what Miss Heller did, I was accepted into the family immediately. She wanted me to tell Christine Heller that Johnnie, one of the young residents who had refused to eat eggs, was now eating them. We talked about food buying. She had decided to get powdered skim milk because protein was low in the diet. I stayed for lunch, pleased that there were no apologies for my cracked cup. The children had completed a plant-pressing project. They were very proud of it and insisted that I take the whole press to show Miss Heller. They were afraid that the fragile plants would get hurt if they sent them through the mail. They wanted the press back, though, because they had so enjoyed gathering the plants. My passion to preserve Native food habits was encouraged.

The Mission asked the home economics teacher to invite me to present a lesson for her class, and so my involvement with schools started again. She had done little with foods and food preparation in the classroom. The lab was equipped with stoves, but they had not been connected. As I had found before, the younger students showed greater enthusiasm and interest in the lessons. The fifth grade had just finished a unit on nutrition, so the presentation reinforced their knowledge; the sixth graders had not had any lessons on nutrition, but they were interested, and the teacher was eager for them to learn the information.

The Kodiak Community Center, where school lunches for the city were prepared, needed help. The wife of the director had volunteered to take charge of the meals. Two other volunteers from the community were supposed to help, but both times I was there, they didn't show up until noon. There were no pots and pans large enough in which to cook for sixty-five people. The program started late in the year, so the food had all been bought retail. The meals served were excellent, but, I thought, too elaborate considering the limited staff, so we talked about a plan for simpler menus.

The center director asked me on my second visit to give the children a pep talk about the large amount of food wasted, much of which I attributed to the number of choices. At that point many of the students had heard me speak at the school and knew me. The amount thrown away that day was about one-third of what it had been the day before. The children were cooperative and willing to please, but supervision was lacking. The lunch hour was a constant hubbub.

I dreaded more school lunch duty after my experience in Anchorage, but I hadn't figured in the benefit of Marion's wisdom and community organizing skills. A school meal cost 35 cents. She recommended to the Red Cross that it pay for the children who could not afford the lunch; this was approved. She also suggested to the health and welfare fund that they buy needed equipment. When I got back to Anchorage, I made the purchases and had them sent out. The dishwashing procedure was inadequate, but Marion was working on a plan for teaching a correct way to wash dishes. The organizers wondered about assistance from the Federal School Lunch Program, so I suggested they write the Juneau office. My lunchroom inspections had made me familiar with the federal regulations. At last I had found some use for my unhappy experiences with the Anchorage school lunch program.

The much smaller Ouzinkie School, also on the island, was having problems with its school lunch, but different ones from any I had encountered before. Mr. and Mrs. Minner, who were in charge of the school, had been stationed in Wainwright and arrived in Ouzinkie after the term began. As was common with many teacher contracts, Mr. Minner served as janitor as well as principal, and Mrs. Minner did all cooking for the school at their home. They were victims of the governmental distribution of vast amounts of food no longer needed by the military. For years, without regard to need or storage facilities, schools, orphanages, and hospitals had received huge supplies of powdered eggs and milk and other foods called "surplus commodities," that is, foods left over from World War II. These foods often had not been properly stored and were stale. Powdered milk came in hard, bricklike lumps, and powdered eggs often arrived already spoiled. At Ouzinkie the food had been stored at the school for several years since no lunches had been served for some time. Many of the hundreds of cases of canned milk had been kept in a warm place, not turned, and were spoiled. Thousands of pounds of flour in the attic were beginning to get weevils. The Minners needed the storage space but did not have the authority to dump the spoiled commodities. They had written a letter to ANS about the existence of these supplies and requested suggestions for their use or disposal, but had received no answer.

Because Mrs. Minner was not well and their daughter had multiple sclerosis, serving a "full meal" (called Type A), which included meat and vegetables, would have been an additional burden. They gave the children juice, dried fruits, and milk or cocoa in the middle of the morning. This was more food than required on a "milk only" federal plan. I approved of their choices. In spite of all the surplus foods that the school had received, I gathered that they were not signed up for a federally approved program and did not receive cash reimbursements.

Mrs. Minner was concerned about the recent shipments of more surplus foods. Besides left over military foods, shipments from government subsidies to farmers were periodically sent to schools. She did not want to see food wasted, but there seemed to be no way to stop such deliveries. The Minners let each family take home a can of spinach on Friday. They thought that the village storekeeper would object to them giving away anything more. They were also aware that they should not give away commodities that could be used to make liquor. Making alcoholic beverages from anything that would ferment was common and increased alcohol dependency.

The plane scheduled to take me back to Anchorage was snowed in at another spot on the island. The storm that had grounded us was one of the quick, wet ones that often blew in off the water. I left the airstrip and went back to the Kodiak Mission. It was much more fun to read stories to the children and join the pre-Christmas excitement than wait outside in the snow. As I watched the schoolchildren, it was easy to spot youngsters who lived in the mission. They appeared well fed and active, but those who lived at home and probably had less food and medical care were likely to be underweight and listless.

As was usual with these quick storms, in less than two hours we were off. Back in the city, I went to the Anchorage Health Department to renew friendships and answer recent requests. I shopped for the things needed in Kodiak and wrote my reports to send to Juneau. These last months had convinced me that Anchorage should be the capital because it is more centrally located than Juneau with better transportation and communication.

I prepared for the holidays and end of 1948 in what I now considered my second home. Although I expected to spend Christmas Day in the Anchorage Hotel, a week before December 25, I met a health department employee who invited me to her house for Christmas dinner. I woke up in the hotel to a gray day and decided that since her house was less than a two-mile walk, I would go. When I approached the comfortable frame house, I could hear voices. I was immediately made to feel like one of the group. Neighborhood couples were putting their meat loaf made of moose on the big table with the hosts' dishes of macaroni and cheese, Jell-O salads, pies, cakes, and cookies. We nibbled peanuts and popcorn with beer and soft drinks. There were several other apparently unattached women, and we all helped with the serving. Since I had come empty-handed, I did more than my share of the dishwashing.

In one corner camera enthusiasts showed their latest slides, the usual entertainment. Even though I had owned two cameras for months, my ignorance of f-stops and lens adjustments made me avoid the photographic technocrats. I chose instead to talk to five men who traveled the territory for coastal geodetic surveys and business interests. I soon learned that I had yet to see much of the real Alaska. I met a young man just back from Little Diomede Island, who later took me to the Valentine Dance. He sent me a huge white orchid for that occasion, but I foolishly didn't protect it from the zero degree temperature and so danced with a wilted, but beloved orchid the whole evening. After the Christmas party several guests walked

Pen and ink drawing of reindeer herd by Wilbur Walluk, acquired 1950. Easton Collection

me back to the hotel, and more than ever, I knew I had the best job in the territory.

A group of us made plans to go the Mount McKinley Park Hotel for New Year's Eve. On my first Alaska train trip I remember how excited I was at the sight of moose that seemed to follow the track. The hotel was open intermittently during the winters from 1946 to 1949 and was inexpensive. Guests were generally from the Anchorage area. The accommodations were far from luxurious, but we were able to entertain ourselves. We found a record player and danced. We decided that it would be fun to ski on New Year's Day at thirty degrees below zero. We found some gear, borrowed clothes from those who had more sense, and stayed out about ten minutes. I didn't drink but had as much fun as those who imbibed on New Year's Eve, and no headache. My hairstyle was changed though: when I left, I had bangs. The barbershop had been left unattended, so we went in and cut each other's hair.

After nearly six months as an Alaskan, I wanted to see as much of the territory as I could and was eager to go farther into the bush. I looked forward to seeing herds of caribou fill the landscape. I had heard that the sheer numbers of their dark bodies heading east in the spring or west in fall made the usually empty tundra come alive. I had found that, from Mount McKinley to Kodiak Island, whether by plane, train, or truck, the diverse beauty of the land, the sea, and the Native cultures and foodways had captured me for life.

CHAPTER 6

On the Tundra, Bethel Area

Leaving the beautiful mountains of the Anchorage area, the plane flew low over the tundra, miles and miles of flat whiteness that was somehow restful and hopeful. Each day brought extra minutes of light. The longer hours of sun would melt the snow from the top of the land, revealing all manner of greens and berries, food for humans who lived from the land, as well as caribou and other animals. Frozen rivers would thaw and fish would run. When the "Starvation Month," February, was over, the land would be fertile again. The bottom of the tundra would stay permanently frozen, furnishing cold storage for foods that would be harvested and preserved for the next winter.

The Whitemen had little or no interest in the nutritional value of the Native foodways. Public health nurses told me that in many of the small communities evidence of Native foods such as tipnuk was quickly hidden for fear of ridicule when outsiders arrived. Tipnuk, a buried fish that had been allowed to putrefy, was eaten in many of the villages. It was probably a good source of vitamin K, but, of course, was called disgusting by white people. In one village, however, I saw many sacks of needlefish ready to be dipped in seal oil and swallowed whole, headfirst. Needlefish has bony "needles" along the spine, a good source of calcium. On the Yukon River it was possible to grow produce such as carrots and beets, and many of the vitamins were retained when they were stored in ice cellars. The Native people preserved wild greens and berries in seal pokes.

When I went west, I thought I would take many rides on dog sleds. Dog teams were the principal means of moving people and goods in the small villages during the frozen months. I had my first dog sled ride when the manager of a children's home came five miles to another orphanage to fetch me. My dreams of flying through the still whiteness with only the sound of "Mush!" were shattered. The dogs were thin and had diarrhea. A tarp covered me enough that my trusty tan parka escaped the flying debris. It was a dreadful trip but provided me with visual proof of the problems the man had with this team.

I arrived at my destination, the Kwethluk Moravian Children's Home, after this disappointing ride and met Dr. Albertie, the Bethel Hospital physician. Neither of us had any idea that the weather would be so bad we would end up staying six days. Not only did this upset our schedules, but we were an imposition to the mission people and used up some of their precious supplies.

Dr. Albertie invited me to sit in on his examinations of the children. I began to see the shocking extent of the tuberculosis epidemic. Some old x-rays for two of the children had recently been unearthed, showing moderate to advanced tuberculosis. When the children came to the mission, their conditions were not known. Dr. Albertie needed to know how those children were faring and was glad to find that they were doing well. The care at the home had rivaled, if not surpassed, sanatorium care.

Mr. Trodahl, the manager of the mission, did not know the history of those two youngsters but suspected some exposure to the disease was in the past of most of the children. He wanted to be sure that the food they were serving was aligned with the medical care. He was pleased but not surprised at the effectiveness of the care that they had given their children. There were thirty-three youngsters there, almost all of school age.

Mr. and Mrs. Trodahl represented the brave missionaries who with their families moved to Alaska, risking their own health, to care for victims of the diseases brought by white people. Tuberculosis was arrested in many of the children cared for in the orphanages. Seriously ill children were sent to the new sanatorium in Seward and other distant hospitals. Most caretakers did not contract tuberculosis because they were careful about sanitation and made good food choices. Even my limited exposure, however, was sufficient to give me positive tuberculin tests for the rest of my life and to prevent me from obtaining life insurance when I first returned to the Lower 48.

Pen and ink drawing of log cabin, dogs, and cache by Wilbur Walluk, acquired 1950. Easton Collection

The Trodahls, Dr. Albertie, and I had plenty of time for lengthy talks about the diet of the youngsters. Mrs. Trodahl was interested in food and anxious to learn about nutrition for her own family of four children. Vitamin C was low in their diet; we discussed the possibility of getting canned tomatoes and canned grapefruit, but they needed many more fruits and vegetables. A few rosehips grew in the area, and some Native greens, which could be put to greater use than they had been. Little land was available for a garden. They hoped to clear space for a bigger garden in the future because they had been promised a bulldozer. We talked about using MPF. The youngsters were given unlimited quantities of milk and seconds on the food, but the amount of meat they needed posed a real financial problem.

Mr. Trodahl wanted to find a source of dehydrated vegetables and make better use of canned goods. I suggested some vendors. They already used dehydrated onions. He decided to cut down on jams and jellies and increase potatoes and fruits. They had a fairly large supply of powdered eggs on hand, which I urged them to use. Mr. Trodahl wished to encourage the children to eat unfamiliar foods. He knew that it would be better to have staff members eating with the children but felt that the present staff would be against it. "It is tiring to be with the youngsters all day," he noted, "and the staff enjoys the mealtimes by themselves."

He was interested in the girls having a vocation when they left the home, and we talked about the possibility of training them to be cooks in hospital kitchens. I reminded him that there would not be many such positions available, and maybe they should receive their training in the mission kitchen so that they could be of more help in the mission itself. Since their future homes were not likely to be equipped as the mission kitchen was, they needed instruction on how to feed their families in the Native environment. He was concerned about how they would live in the villages with no supervision after the isolated, protected life of the mission. They would need help gathering, preparing, and preserving Native foods. If the answer to stopping tuberculosis was better living conditions and good nutrition, they needed to know what could be done with a minimum of resources and equipment, such as one communal pot rather than a six-burner range.

The dining room was used as a recreation room with clean dishes sitting on the table while the children played over them. We talked about setting the tables just before the meal, but that created a problem because the children needed access to their own cups for drinks of water between meals. Mr. Trodahl decided that the only answer was a drinking fountain, so I agreed to investigate the possibility. We talked about the practice of washing dishes in their one large tub, and he thought they could afford a three-compartment sink. I wrote for information about costs and sizes for him.

With a little imagination and careful planning, and not much increase in expense, the food service could be greatly improved. They served dark bread, which was good, but the chief virtue of the diet was the liberal use of milk. The nurse kept careful weight records of each child, and the gains were uniform and steady. However, protein foods, fruits, and vegetables all needed to be increased.

In the mission school the teacher did not seem interested in teaching nutrition. She was, of course, rushed with a heavy schedule, but the nutritionist in me thought she was overlooking information that this vulnerable population needed. I asked her if she would be interested in teaching materials, having "Wheel of Good Eating" posters with me, but she said that she followed the textbook and didn't want any.

One never knows what will leave the greatest impression. Later I found, to my surprise and amusement, that I was not as famous in Kwethluk for my dietetic suggestions for the children as I was for my advice about the dogs. Mr. Trodahl came into the kitchen where his wife and I were chatting and doing the dishes. He asked, "Do you know anything about dogs?"

"A little. Why?" I answered.

"Well, ours are logy and don't pull the sled like they should. We wondered if it could be their food." I knew dogs were a vital part of any organization in the interior, and a poor dog team could completely isolate the home. He went on, "Well, they have some, well—er—other symptoms. I don't know quite how to put it."

I laughed. "Oh, you mean the diarrhea. Yes, I noticed that when I rode behind them Sunday. What are you feeding them and how much?"

We examined the mash. Everything that I had ever known about our orphaned cocker spaniels at home came into use. We lowered the amount of mash for his dogs and fed them more dried fish. In the two days I was there they picked up a bit. The next week I ran into Mr. Trodahl in town. "Town" had five hundred people and was about twenty miles away. He ran down from the Northern Commercial Store. "I've been looking all over for you. I wanted to tell you we have the best dog team around."

The use of dog teams for transportation has decreased in recent years, but the annual Iditarod Race has perpetuated the romantic notion of dog teams as an integral part of Alaska. The racecourse runs approximately 1,150 miles from Anchorage to Nome in remembrance of the original 1925 effort to get diphtheria vaccine to Nome. In 1989, after I had retired from teaching, A. Allan Turner, dean of FIU's School of Health and Human Services, asked me to write a chapter about nutrition for mushers to be included in *The Iditarod Arctic Sports Medicine/Human Performance Guide*. I decided to see if the real experts, the drivers themselves, would share what food patterns had worked and not worked for them. A questionnaire was sent to a list of drivers, and twenty replied. They did a great a job of describing their food intakes for the duration of the races they had run. Using this valuable primary information, my chapter gave suggestions and scientific reasons for high-energy intake during the Iditarod.

I proposed that a training diet consistent with the caloric needs during the race was preferable to the carbohydrate-loading strategy then in vogue. Analyses of mushers' reports of food they ate showed an average intake of approximately six thousand calories per day, 60 percent from carbohydrate, 30 percent from fat, and 10 percent from protein. I suspected that not enough attention had been paid to training the body ahead of the race to digest the large amounts of food needed on the trail. Respondents mentioned the importance of water replacement and elimination, so I addressed those issues in the chapter. I did not recommend the high-fiber diets, popular among health professionals, because of the probability of dehydration.

The twenty mushers listed foods that were useful and foods that were not and explained why they thought so. As with any survey of a small group, it was difficult to generalize because individual preferences were apparent. For example, some mushers preferred salty foods to stimulate appetite; others indicated that salty foods made their mouths too dry. Butter was the most unusual food listed (810 calories in each quarter pound). Such a large amount of pure fat should be tested for bowel tolerance well before the beginning of the race because it can cause diarrhea and gas pains. The list of most useful foods included Kool Pops, canned Pepsi, canned milk, M&M's, fruit and nuts (because they are easy to eat), smoked salmon, sausage, ice cream, and precooked steaks. Sliced bread (tastes like cardboard on the trail) and freeze-dried food (causes soft stools) were among the least useful foods. Some drivers considered candy and sweets to have no food value, but this is not scientifically true when the object is to get as many calories as possible.

The weather cleared, the plane finally came to Kwethluk to pick us up, and I went, at last, to the ANS hospital in Bethel, which served the largest area of any of the ANS hospitals in the interior. I thought this would be another routine visit. The nurses welcomed me, and we found common ground and formed immediate friendships. The

Bethel Hospital's Nurses Home, 1949. Easton Collection

chief nurse and I discussed food orders, the canned food that was available and how to use it efficiently, and the value of nutrients in Native foodways.

On Saturday night several nurses and I had been invited to have dinner by a man at the Civil Aviation Authority. We had walked four miles across the frozen river to accept the invitation when a plane carrying Christine Heller, Dr. Sanstead, head of the Nutrition Division of the US Public Health Service, and Dr. Scott, a biochemist, landed on the snow-packed airstrip. We became a regular welcoming party. However, it took the edge off our hospitality when we had to admit to them the real reason we were crossing the river.

Sunday morning about nine, Christine rushed into my room and said, "Easton, you have five minutes to get ready to go to Kwetaluk with us for the survey." The USPHS was conducting a survey to study overt signs of malnutrition, particularly in the mouth, including the condition of teeth. I don't know why she decided to include me at the last minute, but the days with the research team contributed greatly to my learning. Sleepily I got myself ready, and with no breakfast, made it to the truck in the allotted time. Although it was to be only a day trip, I dutifully carried my sleeping bag, as did the other two women.

Huge ice chunks blocked the river in some areas, causing an over-flow on the shore that froze every night. Because ski planes cannot land on either ice or water, we went to Nupaskiak instead of Kweta-luk, arriving unannounced before breakfast. Schoolchildren ran out to meet the plane. They were fond of Mrs. Esther Snaubel, the nurse, but the last time she had come, she had given them shots, so this time when she told them to go to the school building, they disap-peared. By the time the schoolteachers and principal had helped us unpack our equipment and gathered the townspeople, the children had returned. I was concerned that the research team seemed to have no compunctions about changing locations at the last minute without notice to the villages involved until I realized life was so dull in many places in the winter that any interruption was exciting.

The principal organized everyone into three lines to be examined by the three teams. Dr. Sanstead and Christine were the lead team; Dr. Albertie and Mrs. Snaubel formed a team; and Dr. Scott and I were the third. Each of the doctors had a flashlight and tongue de-pressors, and we three women recorded their findings. The people were welcomed by the team leaders with a smile and a nod, as was the custom of the era for researchers. The residents greeted each other silently, and we spoke to them in low voices. No one was asked to disrobe, but they took off their parka hoods so we could see their faces.

We saw many white spots in the eyes, probably caused by a vitamin A deficiency; bad teeth from access to sugar; and magenta tongues, which showed a lack of vitamin B complex. Though we did not draw blood, Dr. Scott estimated iron deficiency by the lack of pig-ment in the fingernails and in the inner eyelids. He couldn't believe the prevalence of these symptoms. At two-thirty we grabbed coffee, then went back for more exams. About four o'clock we got into the plane and repeated the process at Eek. We were very tired when we got back to Bethel at seven. I had to pack because the group was going to drop me off at Akulurak after the next day's excursion to Chevak, one of the most primitive villages in Alaska at the time.

When we landed in Chevak, all the people ran out in the biting wind to greet the plane. The villagers spoke very little English, but the Catholic priest, the schoolteacher, and one other man interpreted what we couldn't communicate in sign language. The wind grew steadily worse. Hal, the Norseman pilot, at first thought we ought to leave right off but then decided that we had best spend the night.

We again found symptoms of low hemoglobin levels, indicating low iron intake, magenta tongues, and stomatitis, inflammation of the lining in the mouth, but we saw good teeth, even in the children. Many of the women had ground down their teeth from chewing skins, but they had no decay. In Chevak there was no store to supply candy. Today we know that this study and others showed that many of the dental problems came with the introduction of large amounts of sugar into the villages.

We had been conducting examinations for about two hours when we heard an elderly man holding a serious conversation with the interpreter. Dr. Sanstead, who was sensitive to everything that was going on, went to the man to find out what the problem was. The two physicians asked all of us to leave the room and fashioned a space with blankets to examine the man in private. When we were asked to return to our roles, Dr. Sanstead told us that the man had severe pain, and he desperately wanted to be examined by a doctor. Dr. Sanstead told us that the man had a hernia, not strangulated, and that he had every right to expect to see a physician, reinforcing that all of the people within the community could request such services.

Dr. Sanstead's attitude and actions were not typical of many researchers then or even in later years. He provided an example of understanding that I never forgot. When I taught research methods, I always told my students about this incident. He showed us how to use our professional expertise even when conducting research and that scientists need to respect the contributions of study subjects.

After the exams we went to some of the earthen homes where many people lived in tiny spaces, crouching on the floor as I had seen the Indians in India do. Some of the older women could hardly straighten up, they were so used to that position. I offered to buy a wooden bowl, which was used for a common eating dish. I sensed Christine's disapproval, and after I spent more time in the North, I understood her attitude. I am still ashamed that I became one of the grabby, insensitive visitors of the kind who went on treasure hunts under the umbrella of professional duties. Wood was a scarce

Yup'ik feeding bowl, 11x7x2 inches, acquired 1949. Easton Collection

commodity, available only as driftwood, and much more important to Natives than money. After that I never purchased anything that wasn't offered for sale by the owner or artist. I have the bowl still and cherish it, especially after waiting years for the seal oil smell to dissipate.

All of a sudden Hal decided to take off after all. Again beaten by the wind, we made our way to the plane. We took off, and then because of poor visibility, flew low enough to see wolf tracks. I proceeded to go to sleep and suddenly awakened to find us landing on a small frozen lake. They told me it was a lake, but it looked like the rest of the whiteness to me. It was in the middle of nowhere and would be our location for the night. The emergency rations in the plane, dried figs and prunes, noodle soup mix, and rice were stale and inedible. We had nothing to eat or drink because it was far too windy to make a fire.

If I had ever expected to spend a night stranded in an airplane, I couldn't have imagined a nicer group to spend it with. We all thought the situation was a hilarious adventure. We passed the time as anyone who has traveled with field research teams would expect. We told jokes, some of which my mother would have called risqué. We tried to create playing cards from an old newspaper, but the sloppy pen marks and fading light aborted that project. The reflection of the snow kept the night from being pitch black. Trips outside the plane to take care of bodily functions in the fifty-mile-an-hour wind were a challenge. We had to go in pairs and hold tightly to a companion's hand. One of the men decided that he could manage by himself, and when he climbed back into the plane frantically wiping the front of his pants, he merely said, "I faced the wind."

There were seven big people in the Norseman with only four sleeping bags. We women and the pilot were the wise ones who had brought them. Christine and Esther decided that Dr. Albertie would sleep between them in the upper part of the empty cargo space, and they would use their two sleeping bags like blankets. I was assigned to lie between Dr. Sanstead and Dr. Scott. With my sleeping bag beneath us, we lay with our heads at the others' feet. Dr. Scott and I thought we had the worst deal because Dr. Sanstead somehow took the lion's share of my sleeping bag. We two had only our clothes to protect us from the bitter cold floor of the plane. We tried to go to bed at eight, but sleep was out of the question for longer than ten minutes at a time. Someone was always snoring. Dr. Scott and I studied the various snores of the others in an effort to ignore the cold. Bundling without blankets was difficult. Dr. Sanstead thought someone would start looking for us, but we told him not to be silly, no one would even worry until morning.

We thought the radio didn't work, but at nine-thirty Hal radioed blindly that we were okay. He was pretty sure that someone would hear it even though we couldn't get an answer. He zipped himself into his sleeping bag and slept on the bench in the back of the plane. He was later heard to say he never thought doctors and nurses could be such good sports.

By morning we all were tired and unkempt. The plane was frozen in. Hal, with a great deal of advice from the other three men, managed to get the plane free with a pickaxe, the only tool on board. The wind had died down, and the engine started. At last we took off. After fifteen hours and twenty minutes on the tundra, we arrived, dirty and hungry, back at the Bethel Hospital. The big disappointment, though not a surprise, was that no one had worried about us. The airline employees worked until nine-thirty the night before when the CAA picked up our message, but no one at the hospital even knew we were down.

There were many different sets of food habits in the Bethel area because the Yup'ik Eskimos lived near the coast and the Athabascan Indians had settled further inland. This region became dear to me because the people taught me a great deal about Native culture and rural conditions. I saw the most primitive eating habits imaginable in contrast to commercial imports of fresh lettuce and tomatoes flown in from Fairbanks.

The others left that afternoon for Fairbanks, and I was to get a plane for Akulurak the next day. I was thankful for a bath and a night's sleep, but by morning, complete with my sleeping bag, I was ready to fly over the snowy tundra.

CHAPTER 7
Public Health Nutrition, Bristol Bay Area

The wind had died down and the sun was shining when the Bethel hospital personnel saw me off to Akulurak on the plane from Fairbanks. The Kuskokwim River was still frozen in the late winter, but the tundra, still a vast sea of snow, promised a thaw. Greens, berries, game, and fish would replenish dwindling supplies. I knew that Akulurak was located in the Yukon-Kuskokwim Delta where the Kuskokwim and Kwethluk rivers met, but the white landscape below us gave no indication there were rivers.

St. Mary's Children's Home, 450 air miles west-northwest of Anchorage, was isolated and rarely visited. It was one of the few orphanages that served food primarily from the land. I was surprised to find another health department person on board who was also going to Akulurak. We had radioed our changed schedules to the home and hoped we would not overwhelm the staff by having two visitors at the same time.

When the plane landed, Mother Superior greeted us. "We're so glad to see you!" The children took our gear and helped us up the icy bank. An hour later I learned that the Mother had no idea who Penelope Easton was or why she was there. The radio had failed to reach the mission; my letter arrived three weeks after my visit. They did not expect the other visitor, either. Even so, we could not have found a friendlier welcome.

Neither of us detracted from the arrival of the other. The Sister said that the girls were judging all the women from "outside" and were glad that they had two to consider. The younger girls touched our garments and then, shyly, took our hands and showed us their home.

St. Mary's Children's Home, Akulurak, 1949. Easton Collection

The diet of the 122 children followed the Native pattern as closely as possible. Thanks to advice from Christine, the staff and older children had preserved thirty barrels of berries and greens. The next year they planned to put up more greens. They reported a problem with preserving the willows in brine and needed to add more water the next time. The salmonberries were all gone, but they gave me samples of blueberries, cranberries, fireweed, and willow greens to have analyzed in Juneau. They caught and dried all their own fish, made their own seal oil when they had seals, and, of course, made their own bread. The skimmed milk powder on hand was the military surplus kind, hard bricks. The children drank tea and refused milk. By pounding the milk and dissolving it in water at room temperature, they could use it double strength and put it in the tea. I got there at the right time because their yearly requisition, submitted in the winter for delivery the next summer, was just going in. This delivery schedule was more efficient than the ANS one, requiring requisitions eighteen months in advance.

My layman's eye, slightly improved after being part of the USPHS research team, noticed a high percentage of magenta tongues and some dental caries. Many of the children had scabies, impetigo, and other skin conditions. The forty children with the most dental decay went to school at the Mission but lived in the village near traders in communities that followed white foodways. Every effort was made to adjust St. Mary's children to life in the Yup'ik villages that they would live in. They learned Native arts and how to prepare and eat some Native foods.

Sometimes the children expressed a desire to taste food prepared for the staff and different from theirs. In the case of olives, they said, "Whitemen's food doesn't taste good." Mother Superior asked me to talk to the older children in the school and tell them which Native foods were good choices, and if they were going to buy Whitemen's food, what to choose. I asked them questions, and they gave me correct answers because they had been well taught. We had fun talking, and Mother felt that the information was clearer in their minds.

Dishwashing was difficult because the kitchen staff had to carry all of their water. They had decided to try sterilizing dishes on the stove and devised an ingenious plan for making small wooden racks for the metal dishpans that were put on the stove in the dining room. They were training the girls to cook by having each one stay in the kitchen two weeks at a time. Their whole system of changes was cleverly done. The chart was a revolving wheel, and a small ceremony was made of announcing assignments. The Sister in charge of the kitchen gave me several good ideas about keeping foods fresh, one being the turning of eggs every two weeks, and the eggs we ate were proof of its value.

The spirit of St. Mary's and the charm of Mother Superior were hard to put on paper at the time. There was laughter and good fun, great appreciation of the Eskimo and his culture, of the children as children, and of the nuns as people. I loved seeing the children do their Native dances and hearing them sing and give a football yell, demonstrating good blending of the cultures. Playing with the children and talking to the nuns after the daily duties were done were special treats for me.

As chairman of the interfaith council in college, I had visited almost all the Protestant denomination services in Burlington, Vermont, but I had never gone to a Catholic Mass. The Sisters invited me to share their Mass but asked no questions about my personal beliefs. I went to regular daily Mass with the children, but when there was a visiting cleric, I did not attend the extra one. It was still said in Latin in those days, and I appreciated its poetry. The Sisters told me they had trained especially for mission assignments and how lucky they were to be in Alaska. I had great admiration for the nuns' dedication and respected their conviction that they couldn't have borne the burdens, under the most primitive of situations, of caring for these children without God's help.

Later I came to appreciate how unusual this emphasis on Native ceremonies and foodways was. I knew that Sheldon Jackson and others like him had divided the territory into areas to be overseen by different religious denominations. I did not know that the Catholic missions were not included. It appeared to me that Catholic missionaries were not instructed "to civilize the savages" as other church groups were. Although they were devoted followers of their faith and instructed the children in Catholic beliefs, they also showed respect for Native traditions and spiritualism. Many of the Protestant missionaries scorned Native customs and rituals and declared all Native dancing sinful, and as a result, the stories told in dance were lost.

Medical problems were the biggest worry, but there were amazingly few, considering the number of children. St. Mary's was crowded and in need of repairs, but these had not been addressed because of the possibility of a new building. When the Sisters and the priest talked with me, we talked about the food situation as a whole, and the lack of vitamin C foods once the berries were gone. One of the Sisters said that they had lots of lemon powder, the Army type with ascorbic acid added, which they could use. They also planned to add more canned tomatoes to the order for the next barge delivery.

The last night I was at St. Mary's, the Sisters and I talked about local customs. Mother Superior told me how the single men from the village came to the mission to "get someone to mend their boots" as a courting ritual. This custom was similar to what would have happened if the parents had been alive and the men could

Pen and ink drawing of hunter in kayak, by Junior Tingook, acquired 1950. Easton Collection

have gone to them. A man went to the Father, who sent a note with names of marriageable girls to the Sisters. One of the girls then met with the man. No words seemed to pass between the couple. They sat opposite one another but didn't appear to look at each other. The girl made up her mind and said yes or no.

The staff worked hard to equip their children to live in the Native culture, to eat Native foods, and to preserve them. When I left St. Mary's, I hoped that the children would be able to live from the land as their ancestors had and to adjust to the changing world that would surely reach the area soon.

Holy Cross Mission was located 420 miles southwest of Fairbanks. I arrived there aware that since the school had many more visitors than Akulurak, they might feel my visit was an imposition. If they did, they hid it admirably. The Father and Sister Superior spent most of their time that afternoon discussing the food situation with me. They too were sending in their annual requisition and interested in putting to use any information I could give them.

Holy Cross had a big garden and preserved a large amount of fish, so it was not dependent on local purchases for food. They served

Salmon strips drying, 2005. Smith Collection

one cup of powdered skim milk to the children at breakfast, and lunch consisted of bread and Native tea. The children ate a good deal of bread, having it for a snack in the middle of the morning on non–school days and one in the afternoon every school day. I was glad to see the liberal use of bread instead of pilot crackers, so commonly served in the territory. Pilot crackers are almost indestructible and prevent starvation but furnish only starch. Bread, especially when made with milk, contains more protein.

Although primarily a Yup'ik area, many of the children at Holy Cross were part white, and almost all had Athabascan Indian blood, so I found a different child than at Akulurak. Most spoke English well, and their habits were more like the Whitemen's than those at St. Mary's. I grew interested in one of the youngest children, Angela, who had been mistreated and starved. Even though she had been at the mission some time, she ate little and feared strangers, but she warmed to me, and before I left, she looked up at me, smiled, and took my hand.

In Catholic homes and hospitals, nuns were carefully chosen for missionary work. They considered it a great honor to serve in

Alaska. The Catholic Church had long experience in the territory, and funding of the institutions was adequate and dependable. Since Catholic missions had not been included in the apportioning of assignments directed by Sheldon Jackson, they were not imbued with the necessity to teach only westernized language and lifeways. The two Catholic children's homes gave me insight into life in western rural Alaska.

The Sisters and I spent much of our time exchanging recipes and talking about teaching nutrition for the lower grades. One Sister was having the youngsters make a "Good Food House," which they proudly showed me the next day. The day I left, they all sent me notes like this: "Thanks for coming. I eat good food. This is a picture of good food." They had represented their gardens with their own drawings. The children loved raw vegetables and ate great quantities of them. They still had raw turnips when I was there in the winter. At that time of year there were very few vitamin C sources available. Although they saved their cabbage and ate greens in the summer, they ran out of vitamin C-rich foods in the winter. Sister Superior was interested in rosehips and thought that they could put up enough for the whole mission the next year. The Sister in charge of the kitchen had excellent food training, as well as a great love of cooking. The girls loved to work in the kitchen with her because she gave them real cooking lessons.

Sister Superior asked if I would like to talk to the older girls. I said, "Yes," and she asked if community women could come. I showed nutrition filmstrips. The women, many of whom had children boarding with them from the mission because of overcrowding, asked food-related questions, and we had a good discussion of Native foods. I told them about the analyses for vitamin C that were being done in Juneau and that one of the ladies had given me salmonberries for testing. When I talked about rosehips, they all looked blank. I said to Sister Superior, "I thought they grow in this area." She said they did, but still the women didn't respond. Then someone said, "Oh, you mean duodawaks!" Everyone laughed and talked about how much they loved to eat them.

One day both the public health nurse and the bishop came to visit. Trying to stay out of the way, I went to the kitchen to talk to the Sister there. When she realized that the priest who supervised the bread making was ill and the substitute priest knew nothing about baking, she asked me to go with her to see what was happening in the bakery. After unearthing caps and aprons, which the boys who worked there were supposed to wear but didn't have on, she rescued the bread from the too-hot proofing shelves and stopped the electric kneader before the dough got too tough. The boys jostled and punched each other on the arms to cover their embarrassment about their mistakes. Sister helped me convince the bakers to put some skim milk powder in with the flour to increase protein in the bread. In spite of their initial skepticism, they liked the new product so much that milk became part of the recipe. I like to think that I had a small but positive effect on the diets of hundreds of children.

With 175 children, Holy Cross had more residents than many of the villages in the territory. It appeared to be a happy place, and certainly busy. Youngsters of all ages were studying, doing chores, and playing outdoor games. Many of them might not have survived without the care they were given there. Years later I was surprised and disturbed to hear that the young clergyman I had seen work diligently for the welfare of the children at the orphanage had been repeatedly accused of child sexual abuse. Such behavior by a church leader is indefensible.

A few weeks after I left the mission, I had a letter telling me that the flu bug had struck. The staff was busy day and night handing out pills and getting meals to bedridden children. They had decided to keep all of the children in bed for a day and give them pills, hoping to stop the spread of the illness. They were glad that they had sulfa on hand. The situation was critical. Water pipes had frozen, and they couldn't use the stove, heated by steam coils. The Sister was trying to cook for two hundred on a couple of little kerosene stoves in the kitchen and the stoves that heated the two dining rooms. The staff members were betting on which of them would get sick first.

I was eager to return to Dillingham because Dorothy Root, now the community health nurse for the whole Bristol Bay area, who had been in the Lower 48 when I was there, asked me to accompany her on one of her trips. This would give me the rare opportunity to see how one of the best public health nurses in the region took medical care and health education to isolated areas.

We went first to the mission school at Alaknagik. The food manager used powdered skim milk and was interested in MPF. She sometimes used soybean flour. We talked about rosehips. She said the youngsters were dosed daily with cod liver oil, so we were reasonably sure vitamin D levels were adequate. She preserved some berries and cold-stored some vegetables; we were amazed at the good condition of the carrots in the root cellar so late in the year. We had a long talk about food and nutrition after dinner, and the staff expressed a desire for classes for the older girls of the school and the village women, much like what we had held in Dillingham.

When we went to the village school, Dorothy said that the improvement in the nutrition and cleanliness was remarkable. It had developed a school lunch program to teach the youngsters about food and to expand their preferences. The food was either store-bought by the school or brought from home. Clean water was not readily available in the homes, and the children got into the habit of doing without water. On earlier visits Dorothy had seen evidences of extreme dehydration and had encouraged the teacher to start a program to entice the children to drink water. On this trip, she noticed marked improvement in the youngsters.

We stopped at a tiny village and set up a clinic primarily for pregnant women and children in the Moravian church. Dorothy had been there before and came prepared with extra blankets to partition off a section of the pews for the dual purpose of creating a clinic cubicle in the day and sleeping space at night. We carried a bucket for sanitary purposes and had to hurry to empty it early in the morning before church services. There were no trees, and this ritual was public. We had a small paraffin stove that provided enough heat to boil water for washing ourselves, to clean the children's feet, and to make tea.

The clinic for babies and small children was informal. The mothers came in twos or threes, proud of their children. As we examined each child, we were happy to hear so many voices waiting outside the blankets. We weighed and measured the children, washed their legs and feet, and gave the mothers salve to treat their children's skin eruptions.

A young mother carried in her arms the largest baby I had ever seen. His name was Dwight Eisenhower. He was the pride of the village, and four other women accompanied her. Dwight was dressed in a grey snowsuit with a matching hat that had a visor and earflaps. His outfit must have come from Anchorage or Fairbanks since it was made of cloth instead of furs like the other children's outerwear. He was less than a year old, and his chubby cheeks seemed to rest on his shoulders. We estimated that Dwight weighed between forty and fifty pounds. Dorothy did not comment about his weight in front of the mother, but admired his clear skin and healthy feet and coaxed a smile from him. After the examination, we walked Dwight and his mother to the door and waved them off. Dorothy later wrote that Dwight had died from the measles the next summer.

Tuberculosis was in the village. Crowded living conditions and no running water encouraged the spread of the dread disease. We watched an elderly woman, a tuberculosis patient, use common twine to tie wet clothes in the cold wind on a makeshift clothesline only three feet off the ground. I still remember how bent and ill she looked. Another image in my mind is the large sign on the wall of the Moravian church that said in English, "The wages of sin is death." I wondered what message they wanted to convey.

I was glad that Dorothy had to stop in Dillingham after our rugged field visit. She attended the follow-up meetings we had with the classes I had taught there earlier. One of my most pleasant experiences was meeting my former adult class. What fun we had discussing weight gains and losses and the recipes they had collected. It was nice, too, to have Dorothy notice that these women who rarely contributed to discussions talked eagerly. She and I were proud of their interest and practical application of the information.

The school welcomed me like an old friend. Dorothy and I asked students to write any questions and thoughts they had from my earlier visit or facts they remembered about nutrition. All the youngsters remembered what I had taught, or most of it, and showed a lively interest in where I had been. One of the boys remembered that Eagle Brand milk was a good thing to take on a trap line because it didn't freeze. They had ordered colorful posters from many companies and had wondered why there were fruits and vegetables on them that they couldn't buy in their village store. I could not understand why they seemed reluctant to mention local berries and greens. Maybe some critical comments had been made between my visits. They grew enthusiastic again when reassured of the value of familiar foods. They decided to make a botany book for the classroom showing which of their foods were good to eat. Dorothy promised to help them.

We met with the Girl Scouts again. The meeting did not stay on strictly nutritional subjects. Dorothy and I wanted to persuade the girls that homemaking was not a degrading career if they learned to do it well. Dorothy was helping the leaders work on adapting the national programs to be useful for the Dillingham girls.

When Dorothy took me to the town meeting, I heard, among other things, about the possible need for a health council. The people were not sure they needed one, and a committee was appointed to investigate. Dorothy handled such matters skillfully. She did not organize, but was available to give advice. She suggested that the town should be certain there was a need before any more organizations were created. She knew her nutrition information well, appreciated Christine Heller's materials, and helped me plan and make some flashcards with pictures to use with non-English-speaking families. The church-driven taboo of Native dances was not in effect in this area. Dorothy took me to a Native dance where the music of drums was noisy and colorful.

The PTA asked me to meet with them to discuss a school lunch program. We talked about the fact that the town of Dillingham did not have any facilities for such a program, and perhaps education for mothers and children concerning their food choices was needed more. They thought they might be getting a new building. I was quick to say that if they had a home economics teacher, she should not be burdened with a school lunch program.

The Bristol Bay area remained a place of fond memories and lasting friendships. I was glad I got to see Dorothy in action. Even after I left Alaska, she wrote me about the programs we had worked on and the materials we had developed. The lengthening hours of

sunshine and the promise of spring showed me a whole new territory—colorful, warm, and light, with hope in the air. I found the
prospect of going east to the old gold rush area a welcome one.
Each part of Alaska was proving to be fascinating and different. I
wondered what the Yukon area would be like.

CHAPTER 8
Yukon Gold, Fairbanks

In April the days lengthened; each day the sun lit the sky a bit longer, and by the first of May there would be seventeen hours of light in twenty-four. As I traveled, I stayed in boarding houses recommended by health department people and was surprised when I came home from a late date to find the landlord planting flowers in the front yard. These annuals would grow rapidly as the hours of daily sun increased, and in a month or so his yard, like many others around him, would be a sea of color.

Fairbanks was built on a series of ridges and bordered by the Tanana River. Beyond the river lay the Tanana Flats, a plain of marsh and bog that included permafrost and mounds of earth-covered ice. The Flats stretched for more than one hundred miles. In the Matanuska and Tanana Valleys the climate and land were conducive to farming. There had been an effort to make this a thriving farming region with exports to other areas, but as the Palmer gardens near Anchorage flourished, these gardens served only the Fairbanks locale. The reputation for huge vegetables still existed, but I never saw the famed strawberry that was supposed to be as big as a Florida orange. Everybody said that the Alaska-grown vegetables were no good because they were too big and all water. The Alaska Department of Health ran many tests on Alaskan produce, and, as expected, a carrot grown in the territorial sun had the same nutrients as a carrot grown anywhere else.

I looked forward to going to the University of Alaska because I was impressed with the Extension Service publications. Since the university was a land-grant institution, I assumed correctly that there were classes for home economics students, but I saw no evidence of any specific dietetics training. I had hoped to find a program for dietitians because the territory clearly needed them. There seemed to be no connection between the university curriculum and the Extension's useful materials. I found none of the excitement about indigenous foods and Native foodways that were described in the recent Extension publications.

Although I was invited to attend a foods class and the instructor was polite, my position and background aroused no interest in either the teacher or the students. While in the class, I initiated a discussion of indigenous foods based on Christine Heller's research and my recent experiences in different areas of the territory. The reception to my remarks was lukewarm. I wondered if I had lost my touch or if the teacher and the students were just immune to the challenges, rich resources, and career opportunities of the territory. I saw no emphasis on Native foods or effort to reach Native students.

In the city of Fairbanks itself, I found a similar lack of enthusiasm for nutrition information. There were no requests for my services, but since I was expected to visit the hospital and schools in every area I traveled, I went to St. Joseph's Hospital. The staff welcomed me, but was not particularly interested in my help. The Sister who was in charge of the kitchen wanted recipes, however, so her name went on the list of people I corresponded with.

The federally reimbursed lunch program in the Fairbanks public schools was a milk-only program. Milk was served to the children in their classrooms during both morning and afternoon sessions at two cents a serving. Each day the dairy delivered reconstituted dry milk, and some of the children refused to drink it. The overall participation in the milk program was 70 percent. I wondered why they found it necessary to have the dairy deliver reconstituted milk from powder and assumed that there was a storage or labor problem, but I didn't ask.

The economy of Fairbanks seemed depressed, and the city and surrounding villages appeared to take no joy in the coming of spring. Unemployment was high and alcoholism was rampant. Gold rush days were over. Other industry had not taken the place of mining or World War II road construction, which had spurred the building of the Alcan Highway. The highway officially opened in 1948, but the roadbed was so poor that it was unused for tourist transportation for many years. Tourism and other industries had grown up in Juneau and the Southeast after the gold rush, and the prevailing mood there was optimistic. I hoped similar industry would come to the Yukon area.

At Fort Yukon, 145 air miles from Fairbanks, I felt no spirit of welcoming the warmth and longer days. One day I walked down the street, a path of packed snow, and met a man who must have been an authentic, early sourdough. He showed me how he panned for gold in the old days. He shook snow around in a rusty metal pan. He smiled broadly when I asked to take his picture. His mouth was practically devoid of teeth. To his right, a derelict fish wheel was lodged in the silt of the Yukon River and sticking out of the water beside him. It looked like a miniature Ferris wheel with broken baskets. Fish wheels had been used on the river to catch fish, an abundant source of food. Many, like this one, had fallen out of use.

The practice of making good use of natural food resources appeared to have been abandoned. Rosehips grew in abundance as they had in earlier days when the Athabascan Indians ate them fresh and preserved them, but the knowledge that they are a precious source of needed nutrients seemed lost by the time I went there. There were large numbers of homesteaders living in the area, apparently unaware that the Extension Service published bulletins to teach newcomers how to use indigenous foods.

On my daily walks, a huge sign over the door of the Hudson Stuck Mission School fascinated me. It read, "Speak English and Talk to the World." Hudson Stuck was Episcopal Archdeacon of the Yukon in the early 1900s. I thought it was a wonderful sentiment and how it must inspire the children. I didn't realize that the sign meant speak *only* English; this meant they would no longer talk to their grandmothers in their shared language.

There were two government schools in the village, and the two-school system was a problem. The schoolteachers at the territorial school felt that all the attention was given to the ANS School. Nutrition instruction was needed in both schools, and a casual observer could see signs of malnutrition.

The food supervisor at the private hospital in Fort Yukon was interested in teaching nutrition to the patients. She had been a demonstrator for a gas company at one time and had good teaching techniques. She also wanted to provide training for the young women who worked in the kitchen and to open classes to interested women in the community and to groups like the Girl Scouts. I wished that I could have taught some of the classes with her.

Nenana was sixty-five miles from Fairbanks. I went there because the health department had received some negative criticisms of the Garr Children's Home. The public health nurse thought that these reports might be at least partly unjustified and asked me to investigate. The home was crowded and income was apparently undependable. While I was there, the daughter of the Garr family arrived. She talked about the feeding problems of the home without any real knowledge of nutrition. She insisted that she had just recovered from beriberi because of lack of vitamin C. She didn't even know that the vitamin C deficiency disease is scurvy. I couldn't tell whether the rumors of problems within the home were true or false, but it was clear that any change in the food system would need the daughter's cooperation. Local public health people needed to monitor if substantive changes were to occur.

The children at St. Mark's Mission were Native, but there was no evidence that any Native foodways were considered as part of their diets. There were thirty-five youngsters in the home. The staff routinely ate in the dining room with them and had the same food. St. Mark's did have its food problems. One of the most obvious was a large number of disliked food items as expressed by the children. The fact that there were foods being rejected, of course, showed that they had reached a high standard of feeding. The children ate from stainless steel bowls. I wanted to find out where the bowls had been purchased in order to tell other facilities that were dissatisfied with their enamel ones. This carrying of information from one place to another was one of the strengths of my job.

I arrived at the school in the midst of a treasure hunt. A huge freezer held ice cream for refreshments. I enjoyed the party but thought it would have been appropriate to include agutuk, commonly called Eskimo or Indian ice cream. The battle may have already been lost for the inclusion of Native foodways in this area that had maintained such long contact with the Whitemen's culture.

When I arrived at the Tanana hospital, I found an ideal welcome for a dietary consultant. The staff knew better than I did what my role should be, and my eight months of learning made me more useful than I would have been earlier. The head nurse had a list of things to ask me. She knew how the kitchen operated and begged for criticism; she was also full of good ideas. The food stocks were low. The hospital was buying locally because much of the annual order had not been delivered in the summer, as it should have been. I thought there was too little food ordered for the following year, but the variety and apportioning of the food order were well done. The cook, who was on leave, was another problem; the staff did not like working with her. The temporary cook was doing an excellent job, and the nurse and I agreed the substitute cook could handle the kitchen.

The head nurse, concerned, was anxious to have classes for the kitchen help. She and I led the staff to decide that it would be better to serve only half of the trays at a time, and then the food would be hotter. They asked questions and made suggestions about the kinds of food and equipment needed. They hoped to freeze fish for the next year. The head nurse took me into the village to watch a man they called Jap-Haley demonstrate how he froze fish by spreading water on the ground and then putting the fish on the newly formed ice and sprinkling water on them. I could see that using this or a similar method, the hospital might lead the way for the resurgence of use of the vast amounts of local fish available.

Since the meat was dried out, I suggested that the freezers had been kept at too high a temperature. The nurse mentioned that the meat they bought in Fairbanks was poor quality and full of bones. When I got back into the city, I called on the butcher, explained what they needed, and asked his advice on the best use of their money. The efficient head nurse wrote that the meat delivered after that was of better quality.

The hospital physician had an interest in all of our projects, powdered eggs being one. The kitchen had them on hand but was not using them. We talked about oleomargarine as a substitute for butter because butter became rancid so quickly. The new laboratory technician was interested in research and was keeping a list of all hemoglobin samples, which would provide data on the iron levels in the blood of the patients. Everyone on the hospital's staff seemed to want to know what was happening with the patients.

One of the most interesting and exciting parts of visiting hospitals was that I became involved in all the activities. During the Tanana visit the chief nurse said they were having a crisis because the order for blood typing serum had not arrived, and a cesarean delivery was scheduled. I was sure that the Ladd Field laboratory in Fairbanks would help; the technicians had always been cooperative in the past. We sent a wire, and Bob Byer's plane stopped at Ladd Field to pick up the serum. The telegram was apparently misunderstood, and only the anti-Rh serum was delivered. With careful cross matching from all possible donors, the nurse was able to administer the blood, ironically her own. When I returned to Fairbanks, I picked up and sent the typing serum. A thank-you letter followed, saying that because the mail had been more erratic than usual, the regular delivery was delayed. The supply I sent had pulled them through for three months. The Tanana visit renewed my faith in the importance of my job.

When I returned to Anchorage or Fairbanks from field trips, I always had some items to find for people in the field. This was a special service that I could provide. I enjoyed finding the things because I liked to shop and wanted to return the many kindnesses shown to me. Hudson Stuck Hospital needed a new can opener. Was there one that would open #10 cans? After visiting five stores, I found one. Letters from three of the staff mentioned what a help it was, especially during floods when they lived from cans. Double boilers were needed in Kodiak, a wire whisk for Kwethluk, gray yarn for a Barrow nurse, camera filters for the Weather Bureau, a meat grinder and can opener for Fort Yukon.

During long evenings in the field, I worked on specific projects. In the Fairbanks area I made flash cards to help the nurses teach health and nutrition. One card showed a beautiful Native child with healthy teeth. The caption on the back read:

Unidentified Eskimo girl in picture used for teaching dental nutrition, 1950. Easton Collection

TEETH
GOOD FOOD HELPS MAKE
GOOD TEETH
MILK EVERYDAY
FISH EVERYDAY
SEAL OIL EVERYDAY
CANDY AND SUGAR HELP
MAKE HOLES IN YOUR TEETH

Others showed pictures of labels of foods available in the stores, such as canned evaporated milk and canned spinach. These were economical items to replace Native foods that people might not have preserved in sufficient quantities, if at all.

After I moved to Florida in 1950, I had a letter from Dorothy Root, the Bristol Bay area ANS nurse. The Regional Director of USPHS came to Alaska at the invitation of the Alaska Department of Health to help nurses working in "pioneer, isolated" areas. An Alaska field-nursing supervisor convinced the director to include Bethel in her tour. The director had planned to go only to Ketchikan, Juneau, Anchorage, Cordova, and Fairbanks. These were hardly isolated areas, especially in the summer. Two of the nurses pointed out to the visitor that stateside health advice such as, "This is the way to brush your teeth; see your dentist twice a year; wear well-fitting shoes with a good support," wasn't what was needed in Alaska. Simple things like the flashcards were better teaching aids. I gathered the field nurses were continuing to use the flash cards even though the director had criticized them.

Even more interesting was Dorothy's description of the visit by another stateside expert:

> Next on July 30 or so we had a Mr. Joe Smith (a good anonymous name, but true) from a special firm in the west who stated he had been hired by the Bureau of Interior Affairs to evaluate the program from all aspects as to efficiency. An Efficiency expert! So he chartered a plane (guess that's efficient if you are in a hurry) and he and Dr. Googe set out to see schools. He talked to me about three hours while I was trying to clean files and I put him to work so he left. Wanted to know if we felt we were authorized to carry out our intended functions and felt we were backed by the office. We made a few little comments like the government regulations on advertising material for health education and I showed him your flashcards! I explained why actual labels showing a cow, carnation and gold cross were symbolic and necessary with non–English-speaking people. He insisted that it was against regulations to use brand names.

I had not realized that there was such a furor over using commercial materials. The controversy had never reached my office. I used many recipes from food companies, and the "Wheel of Good Eating" was a commercial poster. I objected to many advertising materials because they had little relevance to the lessons I, along with other health educators, was trying to teach. Dorothy went on to say she told Mr. Smith that when a label was used, all the brand labels that were available in the village stores were included, but to little avail.

Again I thought of what Christine Heller had said, that I would learn more than I would teach, and each place I went had made this true. I realized that I was lucky to see so many parts of the territory, all of them real Alaskas. The days were long, and as Fairbanks gardens started to grow, I was getting ready to return to winter-like weather farther north. I wanted to go to Point Barrow and learn to like muktuk.

CHAPTER 9
The Top of the World, Point Barrow

The water was open and whaling season had begun in the Barrow area. Already almost the whole day was light. Heavy fog often obscured the sun, but at least it would not be dark. Snow covered the tundra. The temperature was warming but still below freezing for the high. The first of May was the perfect time to go to the northernmost point of the United States.

The Wien Alaska Douglas aircraft was loaded with cargo, and since I was the only passenger, I was given the copilot's seat. When we crossed the Arctic Circle, the pilot claimed that he deserved a kiss from a first-timer.

There was none of the usual fog the day I arrived in Point Barrow. The local people rushed out to help unload the cargo. The many cartons of candy, obviously headed to a local store, bothered me. After collecting my luggage from the pile of goods and supplies, a driver took me nine miles southwest to Barrow Hospital. At this northernmost hospital I found what I had been searching for since I came north: Native foods being served to Inupiaq Eskimo patients.

The hospital was small. The professional staff, two nurses and a doctor, the cook, and the patients ate at the hospital. The menus, high in protein with liberal use of Native foods, were simple and had been called monotonous by the staff. Helen Simmons, the head nurse, who rapidly became my friend, told the staff that the menu was for Natives and followed the Eskimo cultural pattern. Some of the foods were store-bought and some donated by the people in the community. Both times a whale was killed that year, part of the whale meat and some of the fresh muktuk were sent to the hospital.

The diet of the hospital patients was adequate, with the possible exception of vitamin C sources.

The cook was a shy person, and I never got a conversation started with her. She did well for the needs of the hospital at the time, but Mrs. Simmons and I felt she would not be able to handle the kitchen when the planned addition was built. The current kitchen was not large enough to handle more patients. We recommended to the chief medical officer in Juneau that the kitchen be enlarged with a mixer and an adequate stove for baking added. Storage space was inadequate. The cold room had only a small refrigerator; the ice shaft was too small, so there was need for cold storage.

The yearly requisition was well thought out. This was the second year Mrs. Simmons had written the food order. She was aware that the amount of food ordered would not be sufficient if the annex opened early. However, I thought she was wise to order only the maximum amount of food that would fit in the available storage space and also to keep using the smaller cans because the number of patients was still low.

Mrs. Simmons had a good knowledge of nutrition and foods. She knew that the canned salmon ordered a year ago was not a grade acceptable to the patients. (The nurses had decided to list unsatisfactory food products in the hope that a record of them might be used to help avoid purchasing poor quality items in the future.) Spending money on inferior salmon was an insult to the place where the best salmon in the world was caught. I was convinced that the territory needed a dietitian who could work full-time with purchasing and have contact with vendors in the states. Efficient ordering would more than save the cost of the dietitian's salary.

The procurement of water was an expensive problem with no satisfactory way of sterilizing the supply. The dishwashing process was inconvenient; the plates were wiped with towels and then boiled on the kitchen stove. This method would not work with more patients in the hospital. Using single service disposable dishes would be an economy, but the staff did not want to eat from paper plates.

A wonderful surprise came when I met with Mr. Wilson, principal of Barrow Day School. He asked me to observe the monthly recording of heights and weights and gave me the chance to look at the children's mouths and teeth. Mr. Wilson was interested in food and wanted the school's program to be the best teaching aid possible. He had introduced Native foods, frozen fish, and meat slices called quak to the menu for the first time the year before, and the familiar foods pleased the children, if not the staff.

One fifteen-year-old girl described her acceptance of Native foods at school: "When we start to have quock we have reindeer quock we love it very much. Some quock has a fat. We have a good time, but when our teacher asked us which of us liked fish or reindeer, we like reindeer and some of us like fish, so we have fish quock again. We use to bring our knives or oolu."

Other reports from children like this one favored the Native food culture, one sponsored by a white educator in a school program. I was excited as we discussed the inclusion of more seal oil to furnish vitamins A and D. If a source of vitamin C could be found, vitamin pills could be replaced by familiar foods.

Mr. Wilson was not going to be there the next year. He hoped that more quak could be used and that the new principal would find ways to make powdered skim milk acceptable to the children. He had ordered enough powdered skim milk to be served for six weeks because he felt that the incoming teachers might want to use it first on an experimental basis. He hoped the students would learn to drink the "uncamouflaged" milk. We discussed the cost and advisability of adding molasses if the milk was not accepted plain or adding canned milk to each pitcher of the powdered kind. He questioned whether the value of the milk to their diets outweighed the addition of sugars found in molasses and cocoa powder.

Finding the right containers for liquids presented problems. The children brought their own drinking cups from home for fruit juice and milk, but sometimes they forgot or had no cups to bring. Paper drinking cups would allow all the children to have a drink served in a sanitary fashion. We thought that small paper cups could be used for serving seal oil; the children welcomed the oil to dip their quak in.

Barrow, one of the oldest settlements in the territory, was built on a ridge above the sea. Part of it was still a Native town with dogs staked outside of sod houses. Myths about life in the Arctic, especially about housing, abounded in the Lower 48. In the third grade of our one-room school in Vermont, I was told that Eskimos lived in dome-shaped ice structures called igloos. I appropriated sugar cubes and made flour paste to hold a model of an igloo together. Unlike my classmates, I knew that some Eskimos lived in igloos, but not in Alaska. My brother had been a friend of the Robert Flaherty family. Mr. Flaherty had told him that they imported Greenland Eskimos to build igloos for his 1922 documentary *Nanook of the North,* which had been about Inuit life in Hudson Bay, Canada. The Eskimos there did not build domed ice structures. In Alaska the domed houses were made of sod. *Nanook of the North* was the first full-length documentary, and it received both great acclaim and many criticisms about some of the staged scenes and questionable authenticity.

During my visits to Arctic villages, I found all sorts of structures. The children's homes, churches, stores, and hospitals were generally of wood frame construction, as were some of the family dwellings. I visited people in earthen homes, all of which had some sort of sturdy frame material, either wood or whale bones, and, when snow covered, had the appearance of the igloo that I had fashioned in the third grade. The houses, both wood-framed and earthen, retained heat within the structure, and I was amazed at how warm they stayed inside. The warmth came from small fires or oil lamps and the heat of busy people. The women were working on skins, making clothing, and performing other household chores. The babies and toddlers were unclothed and welcome in any adult lap. Although crowded, the floor was clean and uncluttered. Personal items were stored on benches around the perimeter or on piles of skins. In the center of the room a small fire gently boiled ever-ready food in a large pot. Smoke drifted to an opening in the crest of the roof for ventilation. Long entryways with space along the sides provided storage.

On one of my usual morning walks, I saw a small boy on top of an earthen house with a bow and arrow pointing to the sky. Some older men were feeding dogs and moving toddlers away so they would not get bitten. The youngsters seemed to be cherished and cared for by anyone who was around. I didn't see them misbehave or be punished. I had already heard about the respect for and care of others' possessions. I had been told that if I left a boat or even some small tool on the shore in the fall, it would be there in the spring, though

Sod homes in the snow, Barrow, 1949. Easton Collection

someone might have moved it to a different place if the water had risen enough to endanger it.

The contrast of lifestyles based on affluence was extreme in Barrow. I walked through an area of older frame houses, but the large number of new ones was an indication of the changing economy of the village. Although I did no community work in Barrow, I visited some of the poorer homes with Mr. Hollingsworth when he distributed the old-age pension checks, and so became a part of the community.

The cooperative store was run entirely by Native people, with Mr. Wilson serving in an advisory capacity. Mr. Wilson taught those in charge of the store to purchase wisely, and he thought they had begun to make better choices. However, well-paying jobs were becoming available, and surplus money might undermine his efforts as the demand for sweeter, less nutritional foods increased. There was a privately owned store in an area called Browerville where people were buying items such as candy in large lots and then selling them to their neighbors. Cases of eggs priced at two dollars a dozen did not disturb me nearly as much as the cartons and cartons of candy bars and jelly beans, destined for this store, that had been on the plane with me. The military and government and commercial workers were still present in the area. New people arrived, looking for oil. All had cash to spend.

One of my friends took me to see the famous Eskimo artist, George A. Ahqupuk, who drew pictures of Eskimo life. He was discovered and encouraged while a patient in Kotzebue Hospital. He drew on skin and other surfaces. Unlike when I bought the Yup'ik wooden bowl, this purchase was made from a recognized artist selling his art, and I got a receipt for it. I still have the pictures, one of a blanket toss and one of harvesting seal.

My pilot friend from Wien Alaska Airlines arrived one day and offered me a free ride to Wainwright. He must have remembered the kiss. On the way he pointed out the spot where Will Rogers and Wiley Post crashed in 1935. I had a full day's visit to a fascinating village my travel budget didn't include. The trip gave me another chance to receive warm greetings, this time from the children and townspeople of this Inupiaq Eskimo village farther west on the coast. The children escorted me to the school building to begin my visit.

The same teachers were not going to be at this school the next year, but they planned to stay in Alaska after their leave of absence. They were interested in the school's feeding program. Their system was different from Barrow's. Serving at ten o'clock in the morning, they felt, didn't encourage the parents to skip giving the children breakfast and yet fed those who might not have had any food before school. Cereal and fruit juice or milk were usually served. The morning I was there they had cornmeal, milk, and grapefruit juice. Their dried fruit and most of the fruit juice had been used, though there were basics such as flour on hand because they didn't serve full meals.

Village women volunteered to work for a week at a time at the school, so no food was prepared in the community. The youngsters served the food, and the mothers washed the dishes. At one time they used chlorine for a disinfectant for the dishes, but the children went hungry rather than eat from any plate that smelled of it. After that the dishes were boiled.

The children at Wainwright were excited about having a visitor; they showed me their lessons and danced for me. I saw that many of them had dental caries and skin rashes. Medical care in the community was a living tribute to good public health teaching in the past. Some years earlier, a public health nurse had trained aides, and that knowledge had been passed on to others in the community. Now when no nurse could come to the village, aides took temperatures and pulses, gave advice, and reported seriously ill patients to ANS physicians in Barrow or Kotzebue.

Contrary to the usual pattern in which teachers were in charge of the school, the post office, and the shortwave radio, the teacher here had helped organize the village so that a local man ran the radio. The villagers ran their own store. Food had been scarce in Wainwright that year. There were no whales, and money was short. Mr. Wilson, at the Barrow Day School, told me he had seen scurvy when he taught in Wainwright, and this year, in all probability, many manifestations of malnutrition would be present in the village.

While I was there, I was invited to the women's club meeting, conducted in good parliamentary procedure. We talked about nutrition, of course, and the need for using some of the Native greens. Berries were available, but at some distance. I had never seen a more intelligent, attractive group of women. At a children's party, it was clear that this community enjoyed life even though times were hard.

It was soon time to go back to Barrow, away from village life, to a professional seminar. The seminar was held at the Office of Naval Research (ONR). I toured the facility with a young scientist named Bob. I was able to spend time in the library and labs. Meeting Dr. and Mrs. Erikson was both a social and an educational experience. Dr. Robert Rauch spent time showing me how he was studying the parasites found in whales.

On the morning of May 11, 1949, Bob, who had shown me around the ONR, called to see if I wanted to go to a whaling camp and watch Dr. Rauch look for his parasites. I didn't even think before saying, "Yes." As I hurried to get ready, I thought about the importance of the invitation. I wasn't an athlete so I had concerns about keeping up with the men on a trip over the ice; I did not want to slow them down. I had tasted muktuk by now and knew I could eat it, although once I had described it as lard on rubber tires. Since I had never tasted rubber tires, I don't know that my description was apt. I was prepared to eat anything offered.

No one had told me about the spiritual significance of a whale hunt to Native people. I doubt if anyone I knew, including Christine Heller, understood what whaling meant to an Eskimo. In my later trips, I learned that the whole village got ready all year to be worthy of the gifts from the sea. Preparation for spring whaling began during the dark months of winter and intensified in early March. Whalers showed respect for the whale by wearing new clothing and boots. Eskimos believed that the souls of the animals shared their universe. I probably wouldn't have behaved any differently if I had known this, but I would have appreciated the hunt even more.

I put on the warmest clothes I had. Although the sun was brighter, the snow covering the ground was still frozen in the early morning, and, of course, beneath that was the permafrost. My boots were somewhat waterproof and my gloves somewhat warm. My trusty parka, the one with red quilted lining covered with tan twill fabric, was still the warmest garment I had. I was lucky that the fur-edged hood fit my head well. I got into the weasel, an Army all-terrain vehicle, with the men and all their gear. We rode over the bumpy, frozen tundra until the weasel could go no farther; we had gone a little more than a mile. We walked the last five miles across frozen pressure ridges. It was slippery and hard walking, but I managed to keep up. There were dog teams and other walkers on the same route, all in the best of spirits. Finally we saw the black flag flying, indicating that we had reached the camp.

We could see the steam rising from the partially stripped carcass, sixteen to twenty feet high. There was so much to see that slowly freezing feet could almost be ignored. There seemed to be a mass of on-lookers with cameras, children, dogs, and a whole village of workers. The dogs were staked, straining and snapping. They yelped and struggled to break away from their chains. Some of the men were feeding them scraps of meat. A team just beyond the one in front of us had not been fed. The ignored dogs righted their overturned sled and started a good fight.

Among the group of townspeople were schoolchildren from the Barrow Day School. An eleven-year-old boy wrote:

> The men put the meat on the sled and hauled the meat, after dividing it up with the people. After the men had taken home their share, they haul the meat for the owner of the boat that got the whale. The people go to the house of the boat's owner. They eat the meat and other things after the work.

Muktuk from flippers, 2012. Smith Collection

The meat is dropped into the cellar. The people will have whale meat. On the Fourth of July, the men and women and children will have a good time. The Eskimo people like whale meat. The Brower group got a whale May 11, 1949, and the other group got a whale about the last part of April. The people have great times. The people are glad that the men got two whales.

Sometimes the crowd would break for the men to drag a huge hunk of meat, muktuk, or part of the carcass away. Then the crowd would close in, walking in the melting snow that was now a sea of blood. The pieces of the whale were pulled away, cut up, and put in piles; using some complicated system, it was divided so that everyone in the village got some. The women quietly supervised the distribution of the meat. The Brower crew got the choicest parts, the flippers and tongue, because it was their whale.

Here and there people were eating fresh muktuk. One woman in particular, her baby sticking his head out of her parka, was enjoying it immensely. She turned away every time someone trained a camera on her. Dr. Rauch grabbed a piece for himself and ate it with relish. Small children ran around. Everyone was thrilled at the whale catch.

To Dr. Rauch's great delight, they had saved the guts for him. After making sure the precious intestines were safe from the dogs, we melted snow for coffee. Whose coffee it was, I didn't know, but we drank it, black and out of doubtfully clean cups. One can't be choosy at a time like that. We had hacked a sandwich in two with Bob's knife, despite Dr. Rauch's suggestion that his bloody one would do. I was struck with how funny it was to be eating a lettuce and cheese sandwich, frozen a bit, to be sure, on the edge of the Arctic Ocean at a whale harvest. I didn't know for whom the sandwich was intended. I had not packed a lunch, but Mrs. Erikson had sent one with the men.

I estimated that the whale was forty to fifty feet long, and twenty to thirty feet at the widest. I learned later that it weighed about eight tons and was considered a small one. It was cut up amazingly fast. No one seemed to hurry toward the piles of meat, yet it disappeared.

Bob's commander had given him a bottle to fill with water. He handed it to me when we left. Some stateside college used the water from the Seven Seas as a ritual at a dance, and we were charged with filling it from the Arctic Ocean. I took the bottle from my pocket. By this time, I had completely forgotten how funny it must have looked. I was sure the college students would never know that the bottle had been like a tumor under my parka. We could have more easily filled it with whale blood than get to the edge of the ocean as instructed. At the time I wished we had dared to put blood in it. Once filled, the somewhat heavier tumor was returned to my jacket pocket.

Our intentions of hurrying Dr. Rauch were to no avail, for another whale was sighted. The men rushed to the umiat, skin boats, and set out, but the whales were too far away for the hunters to reach them. We saw eight others blowing far out at sea. Two sets of them seemed to dance against the black clouds. They blew together and sank together, a sight that made planes to Fairbanks flying above them completely unimportant. After half an hour the crews came back, the excitement over the whale that got away turned to the one at hand.

I went into a little tent to warm myself. I couldn't get my feet warm. I held my hands out to a small fire, which helped dry the blood on my parka where Dr. Rauch had rubbed his knife in our excitement over the whale that got away. I felt so much at home that I paid no attention to the fact that I was the only white woman there and I had on wool ski pants. I had a problem for which there was no solution. There was no place that could serve as a rest stop. I had watched the women in their beautiful full-length fur parkas go to the edge of the crowd and squat discreetly. The men seem to gather at another spot with their backs to the crowd. Uncomfortable as I was, I waited for hours until we got back to the hospital.

Inside the tent, muktuk was boiling. People drifted in and out to eat it, drink coffee, and sit on five-pound Hills Brothers coffee cans to chat. Someone drew up a can for me, and I sat. Then several minutes later I found that they were looking for the one I was sitting on because it was already opened. They had been too polite to ask me to get up, and it took me some time to realize they were looking for that particular one.

I went back outside to see the stomach, liver, and lungs and, of course, to tease Dr. Rauch, who sat on the flipper surrounded by guts but no parasites. Bob and I amused ourselves by taking pictures of our personal scientist. As the work slowed down, everyone was watching and laughing at him, but that didn't bother Dr. Rauch in the least. He was perfectly happy and kept cutting away, his hands covered with blood. By now he had enlisted Chester, a Native man working for the ONR, to help cut on the other end. Still no tapeworm, the parasite he was looking for. Bob and I told them there was one worm, but it was keeping two jumps ahead of the knives.

We speculated on the names our scientist was getting from the Natives, for they nicknamed everyone. They laughed at each other and us, and although we couldn't understand what they said, we joined the fun. These Natives were used to crazy white men's research expeditions. Bob told me about asking some of the villagers if they would keep the parasites for him from the seals they caught. The next day he found the women working on the seal meat and laughing that they too were scientists. They were collecting worms!

Dr. Rauch got through the last fifty feet, and still no parasites. There was only one thing left to do, and that was measure the bloody intestines. We thought of many schemes such as grabbing an end and seeing how far it reached toward town and other equally hare-brained ideas. At last Bob paced it off—160 feet. Dr. Rauch decided that there probably weren't any worms in this kind of whale. The baleen strainers were too efficient to let in an intermediate host. The stomach of this one had been empty, but he said that only very small objects were in the stomach even when it was full. We took one last look at the bloody shore, the boat with the brass gun that had bombs in it, and the harpoon built to be hitched to the boat. When the dog teams were loaded with meat and the women perched topside, we all set off.

We stepped aside many times for a team to pass us. It was freezing. The walking wouldn't have been so bad with dry feet and rested legs, of which I had neither. However, the men weren't quite as spry either. David Brower and Chester, like the good Eskimo outdoorsmen they were, outstripped us. David had his hands clasped behind his back as if on a Sunday afternoon stroll. Soon I was warm again, though just a little numb. Once I begged for a moment to take a breath, and my companions said that I had proved I wasn't a sissy. They offered to drag me by the arms, but I had chosen to come, and I would get home under my own steam.

We stopped to help a dog team that had gotten stuck in the rough ice, and I finally got a brief rest. Bob still had an orange in his pocket that he gave to me; it helped no end. The men suggested that someone may have taken the weasel, and that would give us an extra mile to walk. I groaned. I was safe now, because they had already decided that I could take it. In sight of the village, a dog team came by. Most of the teams had gone around the rough ice, but a few came over it, the shorter trail. One driver stopped and asked if I wanted to ride, and I said stoically, "No thank you."

Bob said, "Oh, go on!" and swish, I was on that sled in no time at all. That short ride was one of the nicest I have ever had. I got off and helped everyone tug the loaded sled across a hump. A baby sleeping in his mother's parka, awakened by the stop, whimpered. The meat slid occasionally, but it was still the best ride ever. Two hundred yards farther, we were at the weasel. I thanked the driver profusely and climbed in. David and Chester strolled up and asked if I was tired. Two young girls, who had started on the team that got stuck, came by; they had rested in the snow once and then got a short ride, but they were looking very weary. I called to them, and they climbed into the weasel too. Soon the rest of the group arrived, and we set off for the village.

Back at the hospital we got a quick wash up and some unfrozen sandwiches that had been saved for us. We sat around and rehashed the whole day, found out about Dr. Rauch's freezing finger that he had cut and then licked in the open air, and then we laughed about measuring the gut. With more than four hours of walking and even more time in open air, we were content just to sit and gab, which we did until ten that night.

Mrs. Simmons had been busy all day in the operating room. Another sick patient had come in, so she was just then packing to get away in the morning. I ironed some blouses for her before I fell into bed. The next morning, slightly sore legs, a blistered heel and toe, and bloodshot eyes seemed a small price to pay for the trip of a lifetime. I was glad I had kissed the pilot who flew me to Barrow.

Menu

★ ★

S. S. BARANOF

JOSEPH RAMSAUER *Commander*, U.S.N.R.

Sunday May 7, 1950

DINNER

HORS D'OEUVRES

Anchovy Canape	Celery en branche	Crab Cocktail
Sweet Relish	English Pickled Walnuts	Mixed Olives
Pearl Onions	Sour Mixed Pickles	Sweet Mixed Pickles

SOUP

Macaroni   Consomme Clear

FISH

Poached Alaska Halibut Bechamel Sauce

ENTREES

Boiled Shoulder of Mutton Caper Sauce

Saute of Kidneys on Toast

Creamed Pancake with Honey   Hot Biscuits

ROASTS

Washington Domestic Duck Sage Dressing

Prime Ribs of Beef, au jus Browned Potatoes

COLD BUFFETS

Asserted Cold Cuts with Potato Salad

VEGETABLES

Mashed Hubbard Squash		Saute of Broccoli
Steamed Parsley Potatoes	Carolina Rice	Whipped Potatoes

SALAD

Cucumbers & Tomatoes Spanish Dressing

DESSERTS

Steamed Fruit Pudding Rum Sauce

Blackberry Pie		Seattle Ice Cream
Cookies	Vani'la Wafers	Honey Cream Cake
Salted Peanuts	Mixed Candies	After Dinner Mints
Preserved Canton Ginger	Fresh Fruit	Imported Dates

CHEESE

Tillamook	American	Pimento	Roquefort

Black Tea   Cafe Noir   Ovaltine   Postum

Sets of these menus may be obtained free of charge from your Steward

Menu, S.S. Baranof, May 6 1950. Easton Collection

CHAPTER 10
From Field to Desk, Back to the Lower 48

I would miss the huge orange sunrises of the Arctic. Flying south from Point Barrow in the middle of May was a treat because the hours of daylight were getting longer and the temperature stayed above freezing. Subzero weather would no longer chill my feet. Vast white spaces would give way to green tundra. The mountains were still snow-capped, but the streets of Anchorage were clear of snow, although there were still drifts in shaded yards. I had forgotten how much I loved the warmth and bustle of the largest Alaskan city and the mountains surrounding it.

The ANS Nurses Conference would end my nine-month field trip. After two weeks, I would go home to Juneau and face the huge pile of office work. I was scheduled to give a formal talk about Multi-Purpose Food at the conference. Again, the demonstration technique proved its worth. The nurses were enthusiastic when they tasted it. One suggested that it could be used for babies instead of pabulum. MPF was a well-designed emergency food but never seemed like real food to me. I dutifully inquired about its use nearly everywhere I went and suggested it in some places. The advertised price was still a big percentage of the day's food budget in many institutions, and using it did not further my cause of increased attention to Native foods.

I was on the school lunch panel, but my contribution was small. I tried to make my part practical. My comments were well received without providing any world-shaking information. I thought my stories of children's reactions to the lunches were the reason.

Two weeks was a long time for busy people to be away from their posts, but I enjoyed the leisurely follow-up of my earlier visits in the hospitals with their representatives at the conference, both in the meetings and informal social gatherings. It was wonderful to hear that the cook at Tanana had tried a new recipe every day from the cards I had sent her and that some of the hard-fought reforms at Kanakanak had materialized.

Many of the nurses shared that their patients were asking for Native foods in the hospitals, and this led to an open discussion of foods in their service areas, the cravings of tuberculosis patients, and the practical use of Native foods like quak that could be served in some hospitals. Knowledge of local foods would help the nurses instruct their patients who were going home. We speculated about whether or not Native people were immune to diabetes. None of us had ever seen a full-blooded Native with the disease. I wrote to a famous doctor, Garfield G. Duncan, M.D., and later received a letter from him in which he concurred with our supposition. We were talking about what is now called Type I (insulin-dependent) diabetes, which has been found to have a hereditary component.

The conference reinforced my resolve to write a diet manual for Alaska, which I did during June, July and August. Everywhere I went that first year, physicians had asked for help in planning inpatient diets and for meal plans to give to patients returning home to different foodways. I continually adapted existing diet manuals, although they did not really meet the needs of the territory. I knew that I must write diet instructions specifically for Alaska people. Medical personnel shared their frustrations in trying to give complex instructions to individuals who relied on foods harvested from the land and were fluent only in their Native languages. During my first visit in the Southeast, a physician said he had no idea what to tell a young patient about what to eat when he went home to Wainwright. I wanted to make the information simple, direct, and useful to Alaskans.

Civilian hospitals at the time were not as progressive as the military hospitals, so I adapted the Army hospital diet manual. For example, in traditional hospitals when easy-to-digest foods or soft diets were ordered, all of a patient's food was ground or sieved. Food managers forgot that some of these patients could chew, and for them the pureed foods were not palatable and not necessary. The Army manual was more realistic about patients and did not treat a condition that wasn't there.

The manual was written so that the information was suitable for outpatients as well as for cooks unfamiliar with indigenous food. Under "General Diet" at the beginning of the manual, I wrote, "Sick people need a good diet in order to get well. Well people need a good diet in order to stay well. The body needs many kinds of foods every day. Eating is fun and means far more than just putting food into the body—no one has found a machine or pill to take the place of a good cook."

The sections of the manual were color-coded on the pastel paper available for use in mimeograph machines. The table of contents for the manual explained the code. Type A diets were duplicated on white paper and written for areas where fresh produce was available and the diet similar to that in the states. Type B diets were on blue paper and written for regions where the food was largely preserved, like that of the typical small Alaskan town. Type C diets, on pink paper, were written for areas where the food was largely from the land and for people who did not speak English fluently. The diets for people who were not fluent in English included advice like, "Eat all the good parts of the animals you catch. Livers, hearts, brains, and stomachs are good parts of the fish you catch. Fish livers and hearts are good foods." The quotation did not account for the fact that fish don't have big enough brains to eat. One pink sheet was left open-ended so it could be adapted for an individual diet or condition. General instructions were: "Keep food clean. Do not allow it to mold. Keep it in a clean place. Wash your hands before eating. When you buy store-bought foods: buy spinach and carrots, buy canned tomatoes...." There were three headings with blank space to be filled in by a doctor: "1. Eat these foods every day. 2. Good choices of store-bought food. 3. Do not eat these foods." After distributing sample pages for critiques from my health department informal editorial board, I finished the *Diet Manual for Alaskan Hospitals.* It was an in-house, low budget, mimeographed publication dated September 1, 1949.

Sixty-two years later, I found the manual buried in a box of miscellaneous papers. My copy is probably the only remaining one. It is a pitiful sight now. The once white, thin cover is brown and ragged. The thirty-eight mimeographed pages are held together with three tarnished paper fasteners big enough for a manuscript four times its size. Despite the publishing limitations, the manual received positive responses from medical personnel. For a long time after I left Alaska, Mary Davis, our office secretary, informed me of the many requests from all over the territory for more copies of the whole manual and even more requests for individual diets, especially the ones for children.

While I was writing the manual, summer in Juneau was full of reunions with friends, fishing trips, square dancing, and catching up with correspondence from the field visits. My year's experience made me more aware of the Native people and their leaders in Juneau. When my mother and her friend came to visit for two weeks, I took them to hear Dr. Walter Soboloff, Sr., a noted Tlingit Elder, who was considered the finest preacher in the city. As pastor of Memorial Presbyterian Church, he dared to open his church to people of all races and even broadcast his services on the radio. Many of my friends went there regularly, and one friend had recently been married in his church.

Mother was fifty-eight at the time of the trip, and her children thought her ancient and too prone to illness to travel. She and her friend, Aunt Lillian, as I called her, drove from Vermont to British Columbia in a 1941 Plymouth, stopped to see several national parks along the way, and boarded *The Princess Louise* in Vancouver. They saw a very different Juneau than I had seen. Some local, long-time residents had been their shipmates, and the two ladies from the eastern mainland entertained and were entertained with parties at the Baranof Lunch Room. They were invited to teas in private homes that I had never been to. They were entranced with the museums, souvenir vendors, and local shopkeepers. They walked on the Mendenhall Glacier, saw Auk Lake and Auk Bay, enjoyed the small apartment I sublet for them, and had a picnic supper in a shelter at Recreation Park. I got plane tickets for a floatplane to Sitka, and they saw totem poles and the Sheldon Jackson Museum.

Mother had volatile blood pressure that reached dangerous heights, and many activities during my youth had been cancelled to stay home with her. What her children had never figured out was that when she was having a good time, the blood pressure was always within appropriate limits. Three days before her return trip,

Mother's blood pressure soared. She did not think she would be able to leave. A physician friend at the Alaska Department of Health heard her history from me, examined her, and said since she was going by ship, he thought she would be safe. Mother's blood pressure quickly returned to normal levels, and she and Aunt Lillian continued their adventures on the trip home.

I was glad I could afford the trip for Mother. I had been promoted to Dietary Consultant, Grade 2, and made $415 dollars a month. My 1949 federal income tax return has survived all the moves. I earned $4,751; my expenses included $661 in federal income tax and $61.70 in territorial income tax. One deduction I made showed a new priority in my life. I had learned about the epidemics in the territory and made a donation of $2 to the Tuberculosis Association. My professional dues, $34 for membership in The American Dietetic Association, were more than half my territorial income taxes. I have always kept up this membership, and throughout my career, I have qualified for positions on the strength of it alone.

In late September, I took a trip to Denver, Colorado, to attend the thirty-second Annual Meeting of the American Dietetic Association. I stopped in Seattle to take a train to see my brother Dan and his wife Helen in Bellingham. Before I went to their tiny trailer, I shopped at a nice women's clothing store to get an outfit to speak in. I couldn't resist a taupe suit and matching hat; I also picked out a royal blue, double-breasted coatdress with a light blue hat that had funny felt strings hanging from it to wear for a dressy occasion. Since I had no cash, I presented my paycheck for payment. The head saleslady said, "We can't accept that. How do we know it's any good?" Neither Dan nor Helen could be reached, but I remembered that the Reverend Herbert Schultz, formerly the pastor at the United Presbyterian Church, in East Craftsbury, Vermont, had moved to Bellingham. He hurried to the store and vouched for both the Territory of Alaska and me.

When Dan took me to meet the early morning passenger train to Seattle, we found it no longer existed. I finally convinced the engineer of the milk train to let me ride in the caboose, complete with potbellied stove. I had always wanted to see inside a caboose and here I was actually riding in one with several railroad men who entertained me with their stories the whole way.

When I had planned my trip, I found that there were small, single rooms at an affordable price in the posh Fairmont Hotel in San Francisco. I decided to treat myself to a haircut at their equally posh beauty shop. My hair was always a problem. At night, I wound my hair into tiny curls secured by bobby pins. When I went to college in Burlington, Vermont, I had a series of permanents in beauty parlors. Torturous electric machines heated the hair, wrapped in tight rolls and held by metal clips. The new and very smelly home permanents had reached Alaska, and clever friends spent the occasional Saturday night helping my thick, stubborn hair get some curl.

The snobbish stylist said, "You have a dreadful haircut, but a lovely permanent." He was not amused when I told him that it was one of the new home varieties given to me by my friends in Juneau. I didn't dare tell him that the haircut with bangs was originally from a New Year's Eve party on Mount McKinley. It would have completely ruined his day because he acted as if he was wasting his talent on riff-raff like me as it was.

I never expected that my arrival in Denver would be announced in the newspaper and a Craftsbury friend would see it. The second day I was there, the younger brother of a first grade classmate, called and then took me on two tours of the "mile high" city. We agreed the mountains in Vermont were friendlier, and I told him the mountains in Alaska were more majestic. Everyone seemed to be interested in Alaska, and I got a lot of attention. Although I hastened to make sure they knew I was a new resident of the territory, as the title of my talk, "A 'Cheechako' Dietary Consultant" indicated; "Cheechako" means newcomer.

On the day before my speech, a reporter from the *Rocky Mountain News* interviewed me. On Tuesday, October 11, 1949, on page twenty, there was an article complete with a picture of me in my taupe suit. The headline read, "Alaskan Natives' Diet Fits Needs." The content reflected what I had said, although I think it was a bit more stringent than I was. I had been frank, however, and could not argue with most of the quotation:

> White people, as distinguished from the Indians, Eskimos and Aleuts who are Native to the territory, make up half

Alaskan Natives' Diet Fits Needs

—ROCKY MOUNTAIN NEWS—20

Tuesday, Oct. 11, 1949

The main trouble with the Alaskan diet, a woman who ought to know declared here yesterday, is that every restaurant there insists on serving steaks instead of blubber.

Or if not blubber, at least the seafood indigenous to the region. Miss Penelope E. Easton, a Vermont girl who's now serving as dietary consultant for the Alaska Dept. of Health, admitted that she wasn't very fond of blubber, known as muktuk in the North.

But at least she ate it without grimacing when she had to, she proudly said as she returned from a steak lunch to City Auditorium, where she is attending the 32d annual convention of the American Dietetic Assn.

White Folk Give Trouble

White people, as distinguished from the Indians, Eskimos and Aleuts who are native to the territory, make up half Alaska's population of 100,000—and provide most of the dietary trouble, according to Miss Easton.

They arrive in Alaska with their American prejudices about food, and generally won't consider relaxing them, she complained. Thus they prefer to spend up to two dollars a dozen for fresh eggs flown into the country than to eat cheap dried eggs, which have as high a nutritional value.

Fresh eggs are fine, in Miss Easton's book—but when they cut such a swathe in the budget that other essentials have to be omitted, she wants no part of them.

Shun Canned Juices

Similarly, she said, they won't drink evaporated milk, even though they can't get fresh. They eye canned fruit juices with suspicion, even though they suffer from Vitamin C deficiency because fresh juice isn't usually available.

The trouble with Alaska, of course, is transportation. Some of the more northerly coastal cities can be reached by ship only during the summer, since they're icebound the rest of the year.

And when ships can make the journey, the length of the voyage from American cities like Seattle jacks prices up. The same holds true, of course, for supplies flown in by air lines and bush pilots so familiar in Alaska.

Natives Led Astray

The natives, according to Miss Easton, had a satisfactory diet before white men appeared. Now they're getting into the sugar and white flour habit, and generally aping American eating habits — and anemia and malnutrition are often the result.

White people, Miss Easton complained, don't have enough intel-

—Rocky Mountain News Photo.
Miss Penelope S. Easton

lectual curiosity to s a m p l e the native diet. Here's one menu of native foods she suggests for the white resident of Alaska:

Shee fish steak (white meat, subtle flavor) or smoked salmon strips; good tongue (looks like grass, tastes like dandelion greens) and nettles (prickly when pulled, but the thorns disintegrate when cooked — t a s t e s something like spinach), and, for dessert, Eskimo ice cream—fat beaten into a froth and mixed with water. It's no more fattening, she says, than mayonnaise. Labrador tea, which is an herb, washes it down.

In one respect, Miss Easton declared, the Eskimo is away ahead of his white brother. He eats when he's hungry; as for the white man, "Him funny. Him look at watch to see if him hungry."

Rocky Mountain News,
October 11, 1949.
Easton Collection

Alaska's population of 100,000 and provide most of the dietary trouble, according to Miss Easton.... They [white people from the Lower 48] arrive in Alaska with their American prejudices about food, and generally won't consider relaxing them, she complained. Thus they prefer to spend up to two dollars a dozen for fresh eggs flown into the country than to eat cheap dried eggs, which have as high a nutritional value.... White people, Miss Easton complained, don't have enough intellectual curiosity to sample the Native diet. Here's one menu of Native foods she suggests for the white resident of Alaska.

Shee fish steak (white meat, subtle flavor) or smoked salmon strips; good [goose] tongue (looks like grass, tastes like dandelion greens) and nettles (prickly when pulled, but the thorns disintegrate when cooked—tastes something like spinach), and for dessert, Eskimo ice cream—fat beaten into a froth and mixed with water. It's no more fattening, she says, than mayonnaise. Labrador tea, which is an herb, washes it down.

The article ended with what I found to be an offensive sentence, one I would never have said. I thought it showed a lack of respect for Native people. The Alaskans I knew would never have spoken in such poor English. The reporter wrote, "In one respect, Miss Easton, declared, the Eskimo is way ahead of his white brother. He eats when he's hungry; as for the white man, 'Him funny. Him look at watch to see if him hungry.'"

My presentation went well, and I ended with this statement:

A dietary consultant's work in Alaska, as anywhere, is one of understanding the problems and finding a practical solution whether this involves a cold night in a small plane on the tundra, driving a car with a chunk of ice in the fuel pump, or learning that "duodawaks" are the same things as rosehips. It means a compromise between trying to be everywhere at once and still giving good, lasting service to the areas covered. It means realizing that people in institutions are a part of the community and that they come from and will return to it. It means a chance to meet grand people and learn much. Yes, it may even include a ten-mile rough tramp over pressure ridges of the Arctic Ocean to see a newly caught whale and watch its great mound of flesh be put in piles for many meals of fine eating.

During several return trips to Anchorage and some short visits to hospitals and schools, I worked on a book about Native foods by regions. The general information in the diet manual was not specific enough for the various foodways. I sent questionnaires to each region and started dividing the territory into areas. I consulted with the nurses about the foods listed, and they started using draft copies of the booklet immediately.

In January 1950, I took my first trip to Seward and went to the Jesse Lee Home, which was one of the first orphanages in the territory. Some of the children were not orphans; their parents were in tuberculosis sanitariums in other locations. Most children came from the Aleutian Islands or the Seward Peninsula. A hundred or more children had lived in the home at a time. The managers operated a well-equipped dining room and kitchen. The youngsters took an active part in the cooking, giving them valuable training. My struggles with bread formulas made me especially interested in the splendid product I sampled there, excellent whole grain bread.

Seward Sanitarium was a new government hospital to treat children with tuberculosis, especially ones with complications. The children came from all parts of the territory. I was familiar with many of their home areas and took the opportunity to talk to them about their Native foods. I realized how much I had learned about the foods of the Native people.

The food served in the hospital was tasty and well prepared; the cooks made good use of dehydrated foods. They requested recipes for powdered eggs and milk and were making excellent use of the surplus commodities that had been such a burden to some small schools and institutions. The most serious problem in the ward kitchens was cockroaches.

Nutrition education was needed there, as in all the hospitals. Unless the hospital experience included familiar foods, the patients went home no better equipped to stay well than when they came. One morning I gave a talk about nutrition over the public address system. The next day the children bombarded me with comments and questions. "Oh, here's the muktuk girl!" "Do you really know how we keep salmonberries?" "Have you ever eaten walrus?" "Do you really drink canned milk?" The youngsters thought I was a person "from home" because I had visited so many of their villages and shared pride in their foodways. The questions indicated that I had made a small stride in arousing interest and showing them that Native foods were as valuable as what they were served in the hospital.

Before I went to Seward, I knew that my travel budget had been cut drastically. I suspected that without Christine, who had left the territory, I wouldn't get my share of travel funds. While I was talking to the children at the sanitarium, I realized that my real contribution and mission in the territory was promoting Native foods. I had visited the more isolated areas where use of indigenous foods and living from the land still existed. I needed to work in the field more than in the office. I, a white medical person, had tasted fresh muktuk and seal oil. Not only had I tasted the foods, I liked them. I knew what salmon strips were, knew about putting berries into seal pokes. I endorsed the harvesting and preservation methods and valued Native foods for their nutrient contributions. Young children in hospital beds far from home and the foods familiar to them deserved better treatment. I could help, but only a little, from an office in Juneau.

The eighteen-page *Food Resources of Alaska* responded to the medical community's requests for diet information. The concept evolved from the ANS Conference for Nurses in Anchorage in May 1949. The ANS field nurses, hospital nurses, teachers, and members of the Department of Native Resources and the Alaska Department of Health all helped gather and critique the material. The small blue booklet was professionally printed in April 1950 but was not distributed in its final form until later that year, after I had left the health department. Many medical people on my informal editorial board were already using draft versions the last months I was there.

The surprising thing about *Food Resources of Alaska* has been its staying power. In the spring of 2001, Janell Smith, head of a number of research teams, went through file cabinets at the Alaska Historical

Library to assemble background material for her research and found a duplicated copy of the pamphlet. Finding the material still pertinent, she sent copies to her teams. I thought it tragic that no one had done a bigger, better book in all those years. As far as I know, I have the only original copies of this pamphlet in existence.

The book was divided into sections representing service areas surrounding the ANS hospitals. It took eighteen different descriptions to customize the information for the distinct regions. Native foods of each region were categorized as "Meat and Fish" and "Fruits and Vegetables." Detailed descriptions were included in the four-page glossary. In the 1940s, food categories had been combined into the Basic Seven Food Groups, and that was the system I used. The information in *Food Resources of Alaska* complemented the *Diet Manual for Alaskan Hospitals.*

We often used the "Wheel of Good Eating" because food companies sent attractive posters relating to the categories, but they did not fit Alaska foodways. In the blue book I wrote an Alaskan-adapted version of the Seven Basic Food Groups and listed such items as *"Bones and entrails of fish, entrails of animals"* under "Milk" (for calcium and protein).

Dorothy Root, the public health nurse from the Bethel area and my frequent correspondent, wrote to me in Florida after the book was distributed.

> Your book was wonderful—honest. How did you boil it down to so few words and such a good size and keep it entertaining and more or less inclusive... showed it to Betty [Miss Riley of Kanakanak Hospital] and she thought you should send it to a women's magazine, actually she said to *Woman's Home Companion*, or *Good Housekeeping*. She thinks the States-side people would really go for descriptions of eating needlefish and some of the more repulsive sounding recipes. I am proud of you that you didn't. It would simply be more making fun of exploitation without understanding and valuation of these Native people.

In addition to working on the pamphlet, I wrote instructions to help the nurses order food, but I had no indication that they were distributed. The ANS catalogue of foods that I used changed before I finished my instructions for ordering, but the formulas would still have been helpful. I had a brisk correspondence with nurses and managers of the children's homes, as well as other community people who had taught me so much. But the correspondence and brief, infrequent trips to Anchorage were not sufficient to make me useful to my real clients.

Life in Juneau was fun. I enjoyed the new apartment I shared with another government worker. My former classmate roommate Helen Amos had returned to the Lower 48. I was amazed at how many of the men I met in Alaska were named Bob, and in Juneau a new one came into my life. I looked forward to the single blossom delivered to my office every Friday. I had time on weekends for dates. During good skiing weather, a bunch of us climbed four hours to the top of a ski run carrying our heavy wooden skies and ski poles. When we reached the top after several rest stops, we heated our soup and sandwiches over the fire in an oil barrel at the lean-to on the summit. We softened paraffin and applied it to our skis. Although the jumps were low, most of us had many spills and laughs rolling around in the snow. The trip down, even with these interruptions, took less than an hour.

The dismantling of the Nutrition Unit was left to me, the only nutritionist in the health department. We designed a plan for Mary Davis, the secretary, to keep up with the correspondence. Amid the voluminous papers I insisted on keeping crept the yellow copies of narratives I had sent from the field. Copies of these papers became mixed with personal effects in my old Army footlockers.

When an attractive position in Florida was offered to me, I decided that the time had come to move. I ended up being a two-year employee in Alaska, after I had scorned other government employees for staying the same amount of time. I completed my projects and continued to work on *Food Resources of Alaska.* After several drafts critiqued by hospital personnel, I approved a version for publication. I hoped it would be distributed before I left, but had to give Mary Davis detailed mailing lists because it didn't go out until September.

The publication of my Denver talk in the *Journal of the American Dietetic Association* in September of 1950 brought a flood of requests from government officials and foreign countries asking for copies of everything I had written. Mary forwarded the inquiries to my office in Tallahassee, Florida. I accepted reasonable requests and referred the others to a Juneau office, where I knew they would be ignored.

Friends gave goodbye parties to wish me well in the too-hot state of Florida. I went to the Alaska Native Service Arts and Crafts office in Juneau and bought some of the Native art. Among the most precious to me are four pen and ink drawings. In one of Junior Tingook's drawings, a polar bear with a captured seal looks at another seal on a neighboring ice floe, and the other one shows a lone hunter in a kayak. Wilbur Walluk, who signed one drawing, "Eskimo Artist of Arctic, Alaska," drew a log building complete with a cache and dogs staked in the front. Each dog had a different stance and expression. His other picture depicted a reindeer herd and herder crossing the landscape. In the drawings, I see their love of life in the Arctic.

I had learned more than I had taught. I had gone from the panhandle to the top of the world. I had caught and cleaned salmon, gained respect for rosehips, eaten quak dipped in seal oil, and learned to like muktuk. I cared about Native people and their foodways and wanted them to retain their cultures. I had worked alongside public health workers who tirelessly tried to repair the devastation caused by diseases brought to the land by Whitemen. I hoped that, if statehood came, all Alaskans would prosper and respect each other's food cultures.

Finally the day came when I boarded the *S. S. Baranof* for a taste of the cruise ship's foodway, sailing south to Seattle. I found a dozen roses in my stateroom. When the departing whistle blew, I went on deck and waved goodbye one more time to my friends. Juneau disappeared in the mist, a mist that matched the one in my eyes.

Epilogue

On a balmy March day in 1996 in Zephyrhills, Florida, the phone rang. Janell Smith, a former graduate student of mine, was calling from Unalaska/Dutch Harbor, Alaska, where she had been regional coordinator for the Women, Infants, and Children (WIC) program for two years. She asked me to work with her on a grant to develop a series of television programs and evaluation materials that included Aleutian Island foodways. I immediately interrupted planning for my upcoming move to Fearrington Village, North Carolina.

Admiring her courage in hiring an arthritic, seventy-three-year-old, retired college professor, I bought clothes appropriate for June in the Aleutian Islands and prepared for a return to Alaska. I would be working in an area where I had not worked before. My enthusiasm knew no bounds.

When I arrived, Janell helped me grab my duffel bag and suitcases from the revolving track in the baggage area of the modern Anchorage airport. We drove in multiple lanes of traffic with bright lights and fast food restaurants lining the roadways to the Northern Lights Hotel. A full-sized, stuffed moose dominated the lobby. The Anchorage that greeted me in May 1996 was not the Anchorage I had left forty-six years before.

The epidemics had abated, the children's homes closed, and orphaned children were cared for by their extended families, as they had been before so many adults died from the dread diseases. The foodways of citizens, Whitemen and Natives alike, were different from when I worked there. I was eager to see how the Native food customs had fared. The earthquake occurred in 1964, five years after statehood. Oil was discovered in Prudhoe Bay in 1967, and the pipeline completed in 1977. The *Exxon Valdez* oil spill happened in 1989 and was still affecting vast amounts of indigenous foods in southern Alaska.

The Alaska Native Claims Settlement Act of 1971 affected the legal status and lifestyles of the Native tribes. The Elders of the villages again kept track of where adopted children were living so that close family members did not intermarry. I met several young adult Natives who had been raised in foster families, away from their birth villages. They cherished both their foster families and their blood relatives.

I was a different person too. My experiences included more Army service in the Korean Conflict, marriage, the births of two girls, divorce, earning a PhD, and teaching at universities for twenty-one years. I walked more slowly, and my waistline had increased, but my love for Alaska was unchanged.

Janell took me to meet Dimitri Philemonof, Director of the Aleutian/Pribilof Islands Association (APIA), a cosponsoring agency for the grant. From him I heard for the first time about the Aleut Evacuation of World War II. Even though I had traveled to the Alaskan west coast and had been to Kodiak Island in 1949, this tragedy was never mentioned in my earlier visit. After the June 1942 bombardment of Dutch Harbor and invasion of Attu Island by the Japanese, the United States military leaders decided to evacuate the Aleut residents of nine villages on six small Pacific islands, including the Pribilofs. This move ostensibly protected the islanders, but the St. Paul and St. George islands were included because the military wanted to continue fur seal harvests.

Nearly one thousand Aleuts were relocated to five dilapidated, century-old former cannery sites in southeastern Alaska, over two thousand miles away. There were fifty-nine deaths among the Elders and young children during the three years of internment in poorly heated buildings with bad sanitation and inadequate food supplies. Authorities told men, experts in seal harvesting, that they should return to the islands during the summers to provide furs for cold weather clothing for military pilots. Records showed the skins were sold to a fur company that contracted with the government, making huge profits. At the end of the war most of the Aleut people, many ill and nearly starved, were allowed to return to their villages. Their homes had been looted and systematically burned. Their centuries-old, beautiful Russian Orthodox churches were desecrated; some had even been used for target practice and to house animals.

Philemonof, a young Aleut leader, heard his Elders' tales of the evacuation. He had come to believe the entire episode had been an unnecessary insult to his people. Although the Elders didn't want to relive the experience and had counseled their families to forget about the tragic incident, he and other tribal leaders pursued the matter. Finally, forty-three years after the evacuation, on August 10, 1988, Public Law 100-383 was passed. The United States government awarded financial restitution and an apology to the Aleuts.

At the APIA office the staff treated us to a carry-in lunch of Native foods. The seal oil was fresh and delicate, the fish stewed with seaweed, the fresh herring eggs were on hemlock branches and twigs, and all of this was served with pilot crackers, butter, and salmonberry jelly. A young woman, whose parents had been in Catholic orphanages that I had visited in 1949, told me she made all the bread for her family. Her mother had taught her to put powdered milk in it. I was pleased to know that my teaching had been passed down. I hoped hundreds of children had eaten more nutritious bread all these years because of me.

We were lucky and had good weather to fly into Dutch Harbor. Bald eagles and huge sea bird colonies circled the airport. I saw old gun turrets and other war scars. Unalaska and Dutch Harbor are separate towns on different islands with a bridge connecting them. Janell drove us all over the islands in her new sunset-pink, four-wheel drive truck, her trademark. A Florida farm girl, she could drive any tractor, car, or truck she ever met. I had trouble getting into all vehicles, especially seaplanes, so we carried a milk crate or depended on boosts from behind to launch me.

After taping interviews, waiting tables at senior lunch, meeting Mother Gromoff, who contributed the Aleut word of the day for the films, writing the script, and making a film about Native foods, Janell and I departed for St. Paul in the Pribilof Islands. Everyone was surprised that we left as scheduled because the islands were often completely fogged in. During our six-day visit we did not have an hour of fog. I claimed responsibility for the good weather.

St. Paul is an almost barren island, yet in the summer it is awash with lupine of all colors and small yellow poppies. Grey foxes and cats run wild, but no dogs, so that the seal will not get rabies. The walkways, covered with black volcanic rock the consistency of sand, make a contrast to the low-blooming flowers. St. Paul is a paradise for bird watchers, and in the summer there are many bird watching tours.

I peered over the cliffs to see the Tufted Puffin and Parakeet Auk-let. Historically the great numbers of their eggs have been eagerly awaited spring food. I also saw brown-speckled blue, three-corner-shaped eggs of the Murre, along with others. On the ledges above the protected beach, I saw the huge bull seals marking out their territories and the young bulls being forced to stay on the edges. The females were yet to come, drop their babies, and become part of the harems.

Russian influences were pervasive. The Russian Orthodox Church had established a mission school in 1794. On Sunday we went to Peter and Paul Church, which had suffered water damage and dete-rioration of its artwork during the evacuation. Janell joined the other women, standing for nearly four hours. My cane and advanced age allowed me to sit in the small painted bench at the back. I, like the other older women, rotated the six spaces on the bench and stood part of the time. It was a saint's day, which meant there were three consecutive services. The priests conducted Masses in flowing black robes. I enjoyed looking at the exquisite icons.

After the services, we were welcomed to eat from the dishes of dried salmon, Aleut soup made with corned beef, alladax, the word for Russian frybread, and salmonberry jelly. I told one of the Elders I was sorry that I had not packed a skirt to wear. She smiled, patted my arm and said, "The important thing is that you came."

In the clinic I helped with the children while Janell recorded dietary intakes. When she took blood samples, she gave the toddlers Polaroid pictures of themselves to watch develop. I held impromptu diabetes clinics in the coffee room. We provided toys and animal crackers for the children and grandchildren who came with the adults.

The other kookas, Aleut for grandmother, sought me out and talked to me about the problems of getting exercise in the winters and having enough fruits and vegetables available. Several of these

Elders had been children at the time of the evacuation and talked about the hardships of those years in the rainforests of the Southeast, so different from their home island. These women did not discuss that era with Janell, but they felt free to talk to another person of their age.

Just as both had been important fifty years before, the significance of the weather and bush pilots was clear in these visits. Unexpected, wonderful weather had preceded an earthquake on the island of Adak on June 10, 1996, which spawned a tsunami alert in Dutch Harbor. My room in the Grand Aleutian Hotel faced the open water, but I escaped the wave, as did Dutch Harbor. On later trips, fog blinded the pilot and obscured the Barrow runway; a storm prevented us going to Deering. Mosquitoes greeted us in profusion in the summer and made for discomfort, if not danger. Strong winds drove them away, but the trick was to have enough wind to blow the mosquitoes out and not be subjected to a full-fledged storm. The bush pilots had more regular schedules than in my earlier experiences with them; even so, they made minute-by-minute changes in their flight plans because, as always, the weather was really in charge. The camaraderie of the pilots was still evident. The new owner of what had been Wien Alaska Airlines welcomed me warmly as a return passenger. After I returned to the Lower 48, the local television stations played our tapes over and over for years.

As five years went by, I moved to Fearrington Village, became a transplanted Tarheel, and enjoyed teaching and taking continuing education classes. Then Janell called. This time she was going to study women of childbearing age in five rural Alaskan villages and one urban location. Of course, I was ready to head for Anchorage. She again asked me back for her study of Inupiaq Eskimo Elders in 2004 and 2005. One of the Elders told me that they were the most researched group in the country, and I had no evidence to dispute her claim.

Research protocols had changed since I was a part of studies in 1949. Leaders in the village communities approved research instruments in the planning stages and picked convenient dates for us to come. They appreciated Janell's approach, including having an older person on her team, and eagerly helped her with her research. Janell and I formed the core of every team. Other team members were graduate students in anthropology, dietetics, and medicine. Professionals from these disciplines joined us from time to time. Janell was respectful of the villages' customs and events. Once when a beloved Elder died, she rearranged our whole research schedule on a moment's notice.

In each village, I saw modern school buildings. High school is now provided in all areas, but was not in 1948. Schools had gymnasiums that were available to the students during the summer. Basketball was the chief recreation for schoolchildren. Amenities for visitors were few; sometimes we slept in a school or clinic. When we stayed at a school, we had to limit the basketball play so we could sleep. In clinics we were careful to observe office hours and regulations for using hot water.

Other research teams were in some of the villages the same time as we were. Though led by professionals, they were less respectful than Janell. They thought because they paid respondents, that they could summon a single subject, randomly picked, at any time they chose. The young, formally trained researchers didn't understand why they couldn't fill their quotas of interviews. They didn't know that villagers participated as family groups and found the money insufficient motivation to forego fishing. Subjects participated in our study because they wanted to help us. They knew that results of the Healthy Moms study would benefit the WIC Program. Since we had no stipend to give, we took shopping bags, specially designed and filled, to show our appreciation to our volunteers.

Besides conducting sessions for the students on our teams and making the Research Hospitality Coffee Cake every morning, my real role was to be grandmother to everyone. Word spread about me from the minute we arrived in a village. Airstrips were within walking distance of the main parts of the villages in most instances, but I needed the lift provided by a four-wheeler or the clinic ambulance. Youngsters would jump out of four-wheelers to give me a ride and help me with my luggage. After the rides, they asked each other, "Do you know how old she is?" One of the braver ones, often a ten-year-old boy would inquire, "Are you really seventy-eight?" Young mothers put me in a special category as well. During the first days in a village, I would stay in the clinic waiting room and talk to the staff about our project. They, in turn, encouraged the young, local women to help with our study, and then they were willing to talk to me.

The community churches were important for meeting people and gaining the trust of the village residents. We went to church services, sometimes more than one a week. We sang from hymnals with the verses in Inupiaq. I was asked to offer a prayer for the people at home, unable to attend. The midweek services were informal, with children running around and people coming and going. Some of these meetings lasted nearly four hours. After a couple of hours, our tired students decided that their elderly team member needed her rest and handed me my cane so we could leave and not be rude.

Janell's office for the Elders' studies was at the University of Alaska at Anchorage. When we went to Fairbanks, the main campus of the university, hundreds of tourists with huge rolling suitcases were touring the city and the University of Alaska Museum. The Yukon area that had seemed so depressed in 1949 was now prosperous.

In 2004, we visited six Arctic villages to make plans and test instruments for the study of Elders the next year. We held informal parties for the village councils and women Elders. Young people and office staffs brought the Elders to our gatherings. We served everyone agutuk and frybread while the women shared their stories and laughter. A new Elder and her friend laughed so hard that it took some coaxing to get them to tell the group the reason. As a bride, she said, she had asked the pastor to eat at her home. She proudly served him her carefully preserved greens, but they had fermented. I was finally able to apologize to Native people for Whitemen who had ridiculed their traditional foods. There were tears in their eyes when I said that Christine Heller and I had tried to preserve their foodways and how much we respected the wisdom of their ancestors. The loss of so many of the adults during the epidemics and the removal of children from the villages to go to school in other locations had deprived these new Elders of their foodways and remedies for illness.

When one becomes an Elder in the village, it is a mark of respect and acknowledgment of wisdom and contribution to the tribe. It is the Elder's role to carry the history of the tribe in his or her head and heart. Fifty-five was the usual age for being named an Elder.

On the 2001 and 2005 research trips, our young team members joined in community activities. They learned how to get fish ready for drying, played basketball with the children, and ran in a fun run. The mayor of the village who supervised the run said to me, "You would have run if you could have, and it's the will that counts," and so I got a tee shirt too. We were all welcome at the council meetings, but only I was invited to sit with the Elders at the center table. They gave me the status of Elder, and I was humbled by it.

We did not line up our volunteer respondents as the USPHS team had in 1949, but went to their homes or provided quiet, cheerful places for interviews. We used long questionnaires, sometimes taking an hour or more to complete. A senior team member read them aloud to each subject. Keeping their information confidential was important, and we were careful to show them all our notes. We offered to let the young women in the Healthy Moms study choose fictitious names, and they enjoyed being "Marilyn" or "Jane." The women Elders would have none of that and not only used their actual names, but wanted their villages identified in the reports as well. Janell sent all reports to the village leaders before they were published. She furnished them copies of all publications.

My visit back to Juneau showed me a city of thirty thousand people instead of the small town of eight thousand that I had known. We met with Emma Widmark, who charmed me. She was the daughter of the last chief on Prince of Wales Island just south of Juneau. She earned her master's degree at Harvard and was with the Extension Service. Emma was a leader in the Alaska Native Sisterhood, Camp Number Two, who, with her fellow members, had studied the research instruments and made sure that the words and methods were appropriate for the foodways of the villages involved. Janell was chosen to be a member of Emma's sisterhood and was grateful for the expertise the women shared with her. Emma and I were co-authors on one of Janell's papers.

In Wainwright, word got around that I had been there in 1949. When our research team arrived, some of the new Elders were sure they saw themselves dancing in the fuzzy home movies that I had taken on my first visit and transferred to videotape. These tapes played constantly on the local television station while I was there.

At the lunches in Angoon Senior Center, I met Lydia George and her friends and heard the joys and problems with using foods from the land and the sea. Lydia graduated from Mount Edgecumbe, and her knowledge of the tribes' use of land in the area was essential to document the Native claims of ownership of land in the courts. We learned how much it cost older people to buy gasoline for fishing boats and how hard it was to find people to fish and hunt to obtain the quotas allowed by government regulations. The cost of indigenous foods increased for the Natives with the expense of freezers for storage and electricity to run them. Some were no longer able to sit up all night smoking the fish. An Elder told how her grandson rigged an electric vegetable dryer to make salmon strips so she didn't have to tend fires all night long.

Because food resources had to be shared with tourists and commercial canneries, Native communities worried that they would not have sufficient food to continue their ways of life. One Elder told us, "The fish do not listen to the days we are told we can harvest. We were told we could fish on Tuesdays. The fish came on Sunday."

The traditional foodways of Alaska are important to young people who have moved away but keep their connection to the land and subsistence activities. Those living away from their villages often send their children to the grandparents for the summer. In this way knowledge of the Native heritage is ensured, but these visiting children and the customary festivals and potlatches also drain supplies. These activities are not considered in the quotas imposed by the government. "One halibut doesn't feed many grandchildren," an Elder said.

The contrast of technology and traditional rural life was everywhere in Alaska in 2005. A friend helped us by calling people to complete questionnaires on her cell phone while her husband hand-butchered a caribou in the yard. There were other kinds of contrasts. We visited a nearly blind Elder and saw her use a jade-handled ulu knife as both a fork and a knife to eat her hearty moose stew from a delicate, flowered china plate.

While in Angoon, we met Albert Kookish and his wife, Sally, and shared their fresh dried salmon and pickled seaweed. Albert told us about the shelling of 1882. Commander E. C. Merriman ordered the US Navy to shell the Tlingit people of Angoon, near Killisnoo in the Southeast. The bombardment destroyed the village and killed six children. The Navy apparently thought the villagers were rioting when they were actually grieving the death of a leader. Ninety-one years later, the Tlingits won a monetary settlement, but not the apology they hoped for from the government and the Navy.

The opportunity to attend a nalukatuk, a blanket toss, when we were in Wainwright was a complement to the whale harvest I experienced in 1949. The gathering was in a wide sandy area next to the beach on top of a bluff. It was a beautiful day with clear blue skies. Huge logs, used like benches, were placed in a circle. Their origins were a mystery to me since trees grew hundreds of miles to the south. This had been a successful year, preventing a year of hunger like the one I had observed earlier.

The festivals, held in the summer, followed successful whale hunts the winter before. Visitors filled the village. Extra flights of small planes were necessary. Friends and relatives came from great distances, bringing their coolers to hold their shares of the harvest.

I was invited to sit with some of the Elders I knew and visited with them while admiring the babies and watching the nalukatuk, a modern version of the festival from years past. An author of one of the Barrow Day School stories wrote in 1949 about the celebration from a girl's point of view: "When Nalukatuk comes we always have new boots, snow shirt, dress, and stockings. We like to have new cloth. We always eat muktuk, whale meat, tea, milk, bread, biscuits, and coffee, too." One of the boys also described the festival:

> At Nalukatuk time we go and see the people jumping on the blanket.... The men always go up in the blanket very high. When they finish eating they go on jumping. They always take pictures of them. The men from the camp always come and see the Nalukatuk. After the men and women are through with the Nalukatuk, the boys and girls play with the blanket.

In this 2005 celebration, a young man from the village jumped high and threw candy to the children. After prayers of gratitude, the hunters and their families served fish soup, duck soup, cracklings of

Modern blanket toss with candy for the children, 2005. Smith Collection

caribou fat, slices of muktuk, and frybread. Between each round of food, squares of muktuk were ritualistically divided among the crowd. I enjoyed the muktuk. Janell thought the crunchy black skin had a texture and taste similar to raw carrots. We declined our hosts' offers to take any of the precious catch. We knew the value of their food and hospitality. At the end of the meal, the hosts cut a huge birthday cake in celebration of the one-hundredth birthday of one of the Elders.

Later that evening everyone gathered in the gym for a dance. The men beat sealskin drums to old rhythms, and ladies of the whaling crews danced in their flowered parkas, describing events of the whale hunt with the flowing, metered movements of their hands. When the Elder who was celebrating her birthday stood, the whole village lined up to dance with her.

Janell Smith's studies found that food-harvesting activities are integral parts of good diets and feelings of well-being among young women and Elders. The most used appliance by young women was the electric frying pan, but it was used as a stewpot. Sweet and fried foods were eaten as special treats. Although it was not possible for young families to actually live from the land, they did pick berries, hunt and fish, and preserve food in modern ways. The traditional foodways were still important, especially for celebrations and festivals.

Author presentation, Inuit Conference, 2012. Taylor Collection

These four trips back to Alaska showed me that the love the Native people have for their food cultures was no longer hidden. Analyses of indigenous foods showed the high nutrient value of the Native foodways. Tourists coming to Alaska in 2005 were likely to eat at

Pepe's North of the Border restaurant in Barrow and encounter the word "Alaskan" on their menus only in terms of salmon or halibut. Few, if any, had an opportunity to learn to like muktuk.

My earlier two-year journey, 1948 to 1950, led to my lifelong enthusiasm for Alaskan Native foodways. From 1996 to 2005, I found that Native people were proud to honor their heritage and teach it to their children. On October 25, 2012, I presented a paper, "Quality and Quantity of Food Served in Alaska Territorial Hospitals and Orphanages, 1948–1950" at the 18th Inuit Studies Conference held in the National Museum of the American Indian in Washington, DC. The audience was interested in Alaska's epidemics and foodways during the pre-statehood period. Young researchers asked about my firsthand experiences.

When I remember Alaska, I see the green summer tundra of 2005, as well as the vast expanse of winter white in 1949; bald eagles crowding the sky over Unalaska; wayward moose walking paved roads and drinking from garden fountains. Now parades of lush summer flowers in big pots decorate the street corners of Anchorage. Wildflowers still color the countryside. People pick berries, and salmon strips dry on racks in rural villages. Mist still lies over Juneau harbor.

Glossary

This glossary appears as originally published, including typographical errors, in the pamphlet *Food Resources of Alaska*. It was written to help medical personnel learn English descriptions for Native foods in order to make it easier to prepare diet instruction for Native people. There were many sources for the descriptions and definitions. Some, influenced by Christine Heller's work, were from health education materials sent out from the Alaska Health Department and the Alaska Extension Bureau. Other descriptions came from members of the informal editorial board for the pamphlet, largely nurses in the field. Some definitions were general knowledge.

Beluga—(White Whale) 11–13 feet long weighing 700 pounds or better. The muktuk, oil, and meat are eaten. (See **Whale Meat**)

Berries—are usually stored in pokes or barrels. When kept in ice cellars or where they are frozen, they keep very well. Much of the Vitamin C of cloudberries can be preserved in this manner. They are usually eaten raw with seal oil. Some may be used in Eskimo Ice Cream.

Cloudberry—a berry similar in shape and color to the salmonberry but it grows on a low plant and has only one berry to the plant. This berry is often called salmonberry in the Arctic. Cloudberries are a **good** source of Vitamin C. They should be kept frozen in ice cellars until time for use.

Eggs—the eggs of wild fowl are eaten in any stage of incubation. They are also preserved in seal oil, which probably acts in a way similar to waterglass by sealing the pores.

Entrails—in some areas the entrails of the animals are eaten. The high nutritive value adds greatly to the diet. The stomach contents of the walrus, for instance, contain clams and those too will add nutrients to the diet, especially calcium. The intestines are some-times used for waterproof clothing.

Eskimo Ice Cream—mixture of fats and oils beaten to a froth with water. Berries or greens or a mixture of both are added. Sometimes shredded dry meat is added as well. The mixture is allowed to harden before eating.

Eulachon—fish that are commonly called candlefish because they are so full of oil they can be lit. The oil is collected by just letting the fish drip. Eulachon oil, contrary to popular belief, does not contain an appreciable amount of Vitamin A and no Vitamin D. Its contribution to the diet is calories. (See **Seal Oil**)

Fish—may be frozen, dried, smoked, salted or preserved in seal oil. Fish that has been dead for sometime may be eaten especially in times of need when a traveler finds himself without food. If the fish has no "sun-spots" on it, that is, no burned places on the skin, it is considered edible. (See **Tipnuk**)

Flippers—one of the choicest parts of the seal or whale. Improperly handled, seal flippers cause food poisoning which results in death. The Eskimos believe that the flippers from butch-ered seals and whales must be protected from the sun, for the sun in some way causes the development of the poison. There is also a taboo against eating flippers that have molded.

Fowl—ducks and geese are often preserved in brine. They may or may not be cleaned first. The entrails and heads are usually eaten in stews.

Greens—are preserved either raw or cooked. In some areas the greens are allowed to ferment and mold but it is advisable to keep them cold and free from fermentation to preserve the vitamin value. The greens when fresh are high in both Vitamins C and A. Greens such as sourdock and beach greens are usually cooked before storing. Seal oil is added when they are eaten. (See **Willow Greens**)

Grubstake—the supply of food bought for a specific length of time, usually for a hunting or trapping trip or for the whole winter.

Herring Eggs—are usually "caught" on hemlock branches by putting the branches in the water before the fish spawn. The eggs are eaten "as is", dried, partially dried, or dipped in boiling water. Often they are used in fish stew.

Houligan—(See **Eulachon**)

Livers—salmon livers and other fish livers are good foods and good sources of Vitamin A. The livers from game meat are eaten when free from infestation or cysts. **(See Polar Bear Livers)**

Muktuk—(Stefansson spells it "maktak") is a favorite delicacy of northern Alaska. It is secured from both the large whales and the white or beluga whales. It consists of strips of the whale skin with a small amount of the fat (blubber) attached. Muktuk is eaten raw or boiled. With the white man's influence, it is sometimes boiled with spices and pickled. Usually, however, it is eaten without any condiments. The black part or skin tastes a little like chicken giblets and requires much chewing.

Needlefish—small fish 1–2 inches long with bony "needles" along the spine. They are often eaten raw with seal oil. The fish is eaten whole and must be swallowed head first so that the needles do not stick in the throat. Eating the entire fish adds calcium to the diet.

Oogruk—large seal. The skin is used for boots and skin boats. The meat is eaten fresh or dried.

Ooligan—(See **Eulachon**)

Polar Bear Liver—an Eskimo taboo forbids the eating of the liver of the polar bear. There seems to be foundation for belief that it is poison for when eaten in large amounts it does cause distress and severe headaches.

Preservation of Food—is accomplished in the more primitive villages by the old methods—freezing or keeping food cold in seal pokes or barrels with or without seal oil. These are excellent methods when done carefully, especially if well constructed ice cellars are made. Unfortunately they are being used less and less and much food is being wasted. More modern methods such as canning have been introduced in some villages but they, too, are used far too little. (See **berries, cloudberries, eggs, fish, greens, salmon strips, seal pokes**)

Quak—is made from reindeer, fish or beef. The frozen flesh is sliced into thin slices and is eaten while still frozen and still raw. Usually it is dipped in seal oil.

Rosehips—the seed pods of the rose. Rosehips contain great quantities of Vitamin C even after being made into syrup or jelly.

Salmonberries—the true salmonberry is not found in the Arctic. The salmonberry grows on a bush and has a berry similar to that of the raspberry. It may be red, yellow, or orange. (See **Cloudberry**)

Salmon Strips—are cut from the thick flesh of the King or Silver salmon and smoked. They are eaten at meals or as a treat. In some areas, they take the place of candy. They are good trail food.

Seafood—seafood as a whole may be eaten raw, boiled, or dried. (See **Entrails**)

Seal Oil—is the oil which is rendered from the fat of the seal. In the Interior this is done by allowing the oil to seep out from the fat. The odor which accompanies the seal oil of this area is due largely to the decaying flesh (protein matter). In southeast Alaska the seal oil is rendered by heat. Although there is less odor from seal oil treated this way, some of the vitamin content is lost. Seal oil is a good source of vitamins A and D. It should be kept in clean containers in a **cool, dark** place to preserve its vitamin content. (See **Whale Meat**)

Seal Pokes—are made from seal so butchered that the skin is left intact. The areas where the flippers and head were are tied off and the skin is turned inside out. The pokes are used for storage of seal oil, berries, greens, and fish in seal oil.

Shee Fish—is a white fish with a very delicate flavor and fine texture. It is considered the queen of all fishes by most who have had a chance to taste it.

Soapberries—are found in Southeast Alaska and in the Interior. They are beaten to a froth (raw) and mixed with other berries. Sometimes they are mixed with fireweed milk or with canned milk.

Stews—almost all the food that is cooked is in the form of a stew. Roots, meat, fish, seafood, and other foods, including fish and fowl heads, are all put in the stew. It is thick and comprises the greatest part of the meal. In areas that have white influence, the stews are seasoned, but the more isolated groups use very little salt and almost no pepper.

Tipnuk—is buried fish that has been allowed to putrify. This is probably like the fish used by the Japanese which contributes large amounts of Vitamin K to their diet. (The principal contribution of Vitamin K to the diet is to aid in the prevention of hemorrhages by helping the blood to coagulate properly.)

Whale Meat—is a red meat similar to beef but it is more fibrous. The seal meat and walrus meat are similar to whale meat and treated the same way. The whale meat is eaten raw and frozen, or boiled in a type of stew. White people find it very palatable when braised or panfried. (See **Flippers**)

Willow Greens—are usually put in seal oil in pokes or barrels. They are eaten raw, occasionally a little sugar is added. Fresh willow greens are an especially good source of Vitamin C. They probably retain the Vitamin C when preserved in seal oil if they are kept cool.

Information and Directions for Preparing Alaska-Related Foods

The directions for making foods described in *Learning to Like Muktuk* have not been rigorously tested and cannot be called recipes. Some of them have been adapted and are keyed to modern kitchens; some basic cooking skills are required to obtain acceptable products. Janell Smith helped with many of these directions.

SOURDOUGH

Sourdough Starter

2 packages active dry yeast
1 cup water
4 cups warm water (110-115°F)
4 cups all-purpose flour
2 tablespoons sugar

Dissolve yeast in 1 cup of warm water. Check that bubbles are forming. If there are no bubbles, discard yeast and start over. If bubbles are present, add remaining water and mix with all-purpose flour and sugar. Secure the top of jar with multiple layers of cheesecloth or a paper towel using a rubber band. Allow jar to sit on a counter top to develop the "sour." In Alaska and other cool areas, this may take a week or more. Then cover and store in the refrigerator. Use at least 1 cup per week and feed the starter every one to two weeks. To "feed," add 1cup flour mixed with 1 cup warm water and 1 tablespoon sugar. (Some recipes suggest feeding the starter with honey, but honey contains wild yeast, which may affect future flavor and long-term life of the starter). Never use a starter that has a black, yellow, or red color, which indicates that bacteria, mold, and other unfriendly organisms have invaded the starter.

Sourdough Bread

2 cups sourdough starter
1 tablespoon salt
2 cups lukewarm water
3 tablespoons melted shortening
½ cup or less sugar
6 cups flour (approx.)

Mix ingredients in the order given, adding flour last, using enough of the flour to make dough that can be handled. Knead until smooth and elastic. Place in greased bowl and let rise. (It will take longer than yeast bread.) Punch it down and let it rise again. Mold into loaves and let rise and bake like ordinary bread. It is not a light bread. Makes two loaves.

Sourdough Hotcakes

The night before you want to make hotcakes, add to the starter:
1 cup flour
2 teaspoons sugar
¼ teaspoon salt
1 cup (approx.) water, enough to make a thick paste

As the starter works overnight, it will thin down. In the morning, pour enough dough into a bowl for your hotcakes, leaving a cupful in the sourdough pot. (Set the pot back in the refrigerator until you want to use it again.)

To the hotcake dough, add:
1 tablespoon sugar
½ tablespoon melted shortening or oil
(½ egg can be added if desired)

Mix well and add:
½ teaspoon soda dissolved in about ½ tablespoon water

If your batter is too thick, use a little more water. Fold soda in quickly and don't stir after soda has been added. If hotcakes are tough, use less sugar next time. Your hotcakes are ready to be baked on a greased griddle.

Sourdough Muffins

½ cup whole wheat flour
1½ cups white flour
½ cup melted shortening
½ cup sugar
½ cup canned milk (do not dilute)
1 egg
1 cup raisins
1 teaspoon salt
1 teaspoon soda

Add enough sourdough to make the mixture moist and hold together just like ordinary muffins. Stir only enough to blend. Bake in greased muffin tins at 375° F for 30–35 minutes. They usually bake slower than ordinary muffins, so it's a good idea to test them and maybe bake longer.

ROSEHIPS

Rosehip Puree

(These directions are for Alaskan rosehips, which are very large.) Wash rosehips, cut off top and bottom. Put in either enamel or glass saucepan. Just cover with water and bring rapidly to a boil. Simmer for 15 minutes. Rub through fine stainless steel sieve using a wooden spoon or masher. Can freeze and later make a syrup or beverage. If added to baked products reduce the liquid a bit.

Rosehip Syrup

Collect rosehips after the first frost. Wash the hips, cut off both ends. Cover with water and bring quickly to a boil. Simmer (slow boil) with cover on for 10 to 15 minutes. Press juice through a clean sugar bag, or other suitable jelly bag. Measure the juice. Bring to a boil. For each cup of juice measured, add one cup of sugar. Boil the mixture until it becomes syrupy. Pour into sterilized jars and seal. Store in cold, dark place. Add two to three teaspoons of the syrup to make a rosehip milkshake. Also delicious over ice cream or pudding.

SALMON

Indian-style Dried Salmon

Eskimos and Indians dry quantities of fish for dog food as well as for their own use. Strips of dried king salmon make delicious snacks and are nourishing eaten raw or broiled. No salt is used. Clean and wash fish. Cut sides from the backbone but leave them attached to the tail. Cut each side in 2-inch strips or make cross-wise gashes 2 inches apart. Hang the strips over wooden bars or racks in the sun over gravel. Although flies may be present, they cannot penetrate the film, which forms quickly, and eggs will not adhere to it. A smudge under the drying racks helps to keep away the flies. The strips are dried for two weeks and then stacked in well-ventilated sheds. Spoilage occurs when drying is retarded by rain, and mold or maggots have a chance to grow. Dried fish continue to dry out due to freezing and may be very hard and tasteless by spring. Wrapping in moisture- and vapor-proof paper during freezing weather might prevent drying.

AGUTUK

Agutuk

"Eskimo ice cream" or "Indian ice cream" was sometimes frozen, but it was usually served cold and somewhat hardened. In fruit agutuks, sugar is almost always added. Oils and fats obtained from sea mammals spoil quickly due to the high levels of unsaturated fat. Alaska berries contain high levels of antioxidants, which may have prevented rancidity. Traditional preparation averaged one cup fat for sixteen cups of berries or fish or meat. Calories per one-half cup serving averaged around 150 for berry agutuk and 225 for agutuk with fish or meats, making it more desirable for individuals needing to limit sugar and milk products. Agutuk made with berries also contributes large amounts of vitamin C, folic acid, and fiber that is not present in flour-based desserts. My friends made faces when I told them what the ingredients in agutuk are. I reminded them that many cake icings are basically whipped Crisco-like fats and powdered sugar.

Sweet Agutuk

¼ cup shortening, caribou fat or Crisco
¼ cup sugar
6–8 cups berries
Mix shortening and sugar until blended. If using sweet berries such as blueberries, add
1–2 teaspoons of lemon or lime juice.
This is not needed for salmonberries; they have their own natural tartness. In a modern kitchen, you can heat in the microwave for 45–60 seconds until liquid and some of the sugar crystals melt. Cool slightly, whipping with a whisk. Pour in berries and mix well. Serve warm on pound cake, or chilled in parfait glasses.

FRYBREAD

Alaskan Frybread

In the Aleutian Islands there is a long history of bread dough fried in seal oil. Called alladax, it is served hot, sprinkled with sugar and cinnamon, or served cold like sliced bread. Alaskan frybread has more sugar and fat in it than frybread served at many festivals in the Lower 48. The higher fat may keep the bread soft in the dry Alaska climate. Alaskan frybread can be made from any yeast dough recipe such as the one below:

1 cup of milk, lukewarm (made with 1/4 cup instant dry milk and lukewarm water)
2 teaspoons yeast or 1 envelope
2 tablespoons sugar
1/2 teaspoon salt
3–4 cups flour
Shortening or oil for frying
Sprinkle yeast over the milk. To make sure the yeast is alive, wait a few minutes to see if the mixture bubbles. Add the sugar and salt

to the milk and then stir in about ⅓ of the flour. Add the rest of the flour more slowly until the mixture is thick. Turn onto a flat surface that has been dusted with flour, knead until smooth. Put in a greased bowl, cover to let rise about an hour. Make pieces in desired shape from balls of dough. If you want flat pieces, pat into a round ball and stretch to make a thin cake. Let the pieces rest while you heat the oil. The frying fat should be about three inches deep. Fry until brown, turning once. Drain on a paper towel and serve or cover with towels until ready to serve. Makes about eight pieces.

Research Hospitality Coffee Cake

Coffee cake was a part of the research projects in small Alaskan villages from 2001 to 2006. I usually made at least one recipe every morning to show our appreciation to the people who shared their lives with us and told us about their foodways. We served it in the morning with tea or coffee when people were waiting for interviews and carried it in aluminum foil to the houses. I often made another recipe in the afternoon for visitors.

1. Find a suitable baking dish. For three cups of baking mix you would need two pie pans or a foil pan—an 8-inch square is a little small, but you can bake a taste cake in a custard dish with the extra batter. Grease the pan with cooking spray, cooking oil, or margarine. Preheat oven to 350° F.
2. You will need a measuring cup, large and small bowls, or even saucepans, and a large spoon.
3. The flour can be self-rising, pancake mix, ordinary white flour, or biscuit mix; whole wheat (or part whole wheat) gives a chewier cake. Put 2½ cups of the flour or mix in the large bowl and another ½ cup in the small bowl for the topping.
4. Put ¾ to 1 cup of sugar in with the flour. Plain old white sugar does well but you can use brown, or if you want, add honey or maple syrup to the liquid.
5. Put ½ cup sugar in the small dish with the flour. This is for the topping.

6. In another bowl, measure a cup of liquid, either water, if you are using powdered milk and have added it to the flour, or diluted evaporated or ordinary milk, if not. Add egg or eggs if you want to use them; you could add reconstituted powdered eggs if so inclined. Beat the eggs with a fork, add enough oil, melted margarine, or butter to make 1½ cups of liquid. After a few tries you will find out how thick you want it.

7. Take the small dish of flour and sugar and add 1 tablespoon of cinnamon. Make the mixture into a thin paste with soft margarine or butter or even a small amount of cooking oil. If you want to add chopped nuts or seeds, go ahead; for fruit, add blueberries or dried fruit with the flour.

8. Now pour your 1½ cups of liquid into the flour mixture and stir a little. Do not beat it; tiny lumps are fine. (If you did add extra sugar, eggs, and oil, you can beat more because it is like a cake.)

9. Pour the batter into the pan(s). Put little bits of topping all over the cake and bake (probably 25 minutes). Test by sticking a toothpick in the middle to see if it comes out clean. You can use your finger and press the top if you are a somewhat experienced cook, but watch the topping because it can burn. Enjoy. It is a very flexible recipe and can be used for breakfast, or with some added sugar and a bit more liquid it becomes a dessert to serve with sliced strawberries or ice cream.

Description of *Food Resources of Alaska* and Recommended Dietary Patterns

SERVICE AREAS

The hospital service areas listed in *Food Resources of Alaska* pamphlet were designed to help medical personnel understand the indigenous foods their patients ate so they could give dietary instructions when the patients went home. Nurses and other educators found the information useful because there was no area-specific food reference available. The areas were: Aleutian Peninsula and Chain; Barrow; Bethel, including Lower Yukon, Lower Kuskokwim Coast, Nunivak Island, and Upper Kuskokwim; Bristol Bay; Juneau and Southeast Alaska; Kodiak Island; Kotzebue; Nome and Unalakleet, including St. Lawrence, Little Diomede, and King Islands; Railroad-Highway; and Upper Yukon.

It took eighteen different descriptions to customize the information for the distinct regions. The basic information was organized with a short description of each area, of the population, of the local industries, and the kinds of food available. Native foods of the region were categorized as "Meat and Fish" and "Fruits and Vegetables." Information in the *Food Resources of Alaska* complemented the *Diet Manual for Alaskan Hospitals*.

RECOMMENDED DIETARY PATTERNS

The US government has distributed dietary guidelines since 1916. Foods were organized in various ways; one even had fourteen groups. In the 1940s, food categories had been combined into the "Basic Seven Foods." In my opinion it was a good model, and the one I used. We often called it the "Wheel of Good Eating." In 1956, a more simplified approach, the "Basic Four Foods" was adopted. The "Food Pyramid" was launched in 1992. I considered the latter system difficult for people to follow and for professionals to use as an evaluation tool. In 2011, a newly developed "Food Plate" was introduced, an updated "Basic Four." The "Food Plate" is simpler and more graphically attractive than its immediate predecessor, the pyramid. Included in *Food Resources of Alaska* was the following adaptation:

BASIC SEVEN FOODS IN ALASKA

I.   LEAFY GREEN OR YELLOW VEGETABLES (for vitamin A)
  a. Fresh or preserved Native greens
  b. Salmonberries
  c. Canned carrots, sweet potatoes, or squash

II.   CITRUS FRUIT (for vitamin C)
  a. Rosehips
  b. Cloudberries
  c. Fresh raw greens and berries
  d. Willow greens
  e. Canned oranges, tomatoes, or grapefruit
  f. Canned orange, tomato, or grapefruit juice

III.   OTHER FRUITS AND VEGETABLES (for other vitamins and minerals)
  a. All greens, berries, roots, seaweed
  b. Canned fruits and vegetables

IV.   MILK (for calcium and protein)
  a. Canned milk (evaporated)
  b. Powdered whole milk
  c. Powdered skim milk
  d. Bones and entrails of fish, entrails of animals

V.   MEAT, POULTRY, FISH, EGGS, BEANS (for protein)
   a. Game meats and entrails
   b. Fish and entrails, especially livers
   c. Sea foods
   d. Fresh or powdered eggs, birds' eggs, dried beans, peas, peanut butter

VI.   WHOLE GRAINS (for vitamin B)
   a. Whole grain flours and cereals, especially oatmeal
   b. Enriched flour and cereals

VII.   FATS (for vitamin A and calories)
   a. Seal oil and fish livers
   b. Fortified margarine or butter

The complete *Food Resources of Alaska* pamphlet is available for download on *Learning to Like Muktuk*'s web page at www.osupress. oregonstate.edu.

APPENDIX C

Nutrition Science, 1948 to 1950, and Research Procedures, 1949 and 2001

In the World War II era, research on the contributions of vitamins and minerals increased, but many of the findings hadn't been published and were not taught in my college years. The high number of malnourished military recruits spawned concern about the presence of nutritional deficiencies in population groups as a whole. Information about symptoms of deficiencies increased with many screening projects. In Alaska, most studies recorded visually discernible symptoms, as in the United States Public Health Service study that I joined in 1949.

The main concern of this large multi-site Alaskan USPHS study was dental health, specifically determining the cause of cavities and teeth lost to decay. Although I never saw published results, current knowledge about the relationship of sugar to dental caries was partly based on these studies.

I have reviewed the knowledge in textbooks of the time, which were the foundation of the project I joined briefly; the diagnoses were based on observations and crude tests. We took no blood samples and did no examinations of the bodies except what could be seen without asking patients to disrobe. My college text, published in 1937, *Chemistry of Food and Nutrition*, by Henry C. Sherman, PhD, ScD, listed the importance of iron and copper in hemoglobin formation. In the USHPS study, we estimated deficiency of iron by the lack of pigment in the fingernails and in the inner eyelids.

Vitamin A and its precursors were known. Deficiency symptoms showed stunted growth, development of eye disorders including ophthalmia (eye inflammation), xerophthalmia (severe dry eyes), or keratomalacia (clouding of the cornea due to the severe dry eyes of Vitamin A deficiency).

Dr. Sherman discussed the "antineuritic" vitamin, which he called vitamin B or sometimes vitamin B1 (now known as thiamin). Beriberi was its deficiency disease. Vitamin B was also identified as important in gastrointestinal activity, growth, appetite, and general vigor. Sherman discussed the concept of the vitamin B-complex, which included other vitamins with different functions. He identified vitamin G (B2) as lactoflavin (now known as riboflavin). Dr. Sherman wrote that there were probably more vitamins in the B-complex. He indicated that poor mouth tissue health, magenta tongues, and swollen gums were all due to lack of some part of the vitamin B-complex because of low intakes of vegetable and protein foods.

Vitamin C received much attention because it was known as a water-soluble vitamin destroyed by exposure to air and heat. Incidences of scurvy, the deficiency disease of vitamin C, were found in Alaska, especially in the spring. Visual symptoms were petechial hemorrhages, easy bruising, loose teeth, and spongy gums. The presence of sallow, muddy complexions was difficult to assess in Native people, but we were able to determine, with the help of an interpreter, loss of energy and fleeting pains in the joints and limbs.

The methods used in the USPHS study were typical of the era. Indigenous populations were examined without their consent and given no remuneration or sign of appreciation. Findings of the studies were not reported to the communities as far as I knew. The change of sites, dictated by the weather, was common. I understood that Dr. Sanstead's insistence on examining the man who wanted to see a physician was unusual.

When I returned to Alaska in 2001, I found a very different research climate, one that embodied the kinds of reforms that many public health professionals and I had advocated in our classes in research methods.

The 2001 project was called the Healthy Moms Study and sought to examine factors that influence body weight in Alaskan women of childbearing age. The study was funded by the United States Department of Agriculture. The research protocol involved measurements of height, weight, percent body fat, and finger-stick determinations of hemoglobin and cholesterol. Calculation of BMI, twenty-four-hour food intake, and frequency of food intake in key nutrient groups was also completed.

This study embodied Dr. Janell Smith's philosophy of participation of everyone concerned. Her procedure reflected the newly published rules for ethical research among Alaska Native populations:

1. Native experts helped in developing the study protocol and the research instruments.
2. After the grant was awarded, a sign was posted at a statewide health event requesting villages to volunteer to participate in the study.
3. Rural partners were chosen to include five different areas of the state, and attention given to the scheduled activities of the villages involved. Local reviewing boards were contacted before the research began. Community leaders and village councils were involved throughout the project. For example, when our team of four arrived at one place ready to start our study the next day, the hospital board had concerns not previously addressed, and a meeting was scheduled late in the day.
4. Relatives and friends provided transportation to the interview sites, helped older people climb stairs if necessary, and made home-visit appointments.
5. The interviews were conducted with a professional team member reading the items and recording the results. All written notes were shown to participants and were private. We assured each participant that if we suspected any health problem, we would notify clinic personnel. Participants were offered the option of using an assumed name.
6. After the data were studied, preliminary reports were sent back to each village to be approved before publication. Copies of final publications were provided to village councils.

The general research atmosphere was the same for the Native Elders study (2005–2006) funded by the National Science Foundation. We examined the role of traditional foods in their view of their own well-being. We had a long interview with the Elders, and they took the opportunity to educate us on issues they felt were important concerning food for themselves and their communities.

Janell had nine articles published in peer-reviewed journals from 2001 to 2009 presenting the research that she did in Alaska. I was one of her coauthors on seven of the papers.

References

"Alaskan Natives' Diet Fits Needs." *Rocky Mountain News*, October 11, 1949.

Blackman, Margaret B. *Sadie Brower Neakok*. Seattle: University of Washington Press, 1989.

Easton, P. "Quality and Quantity of Food Served in Alaska Territorial Hospitals and Orphanages, 1948-1950." *International Journal of Circumpolar Health*, no. 1 (2013): 839.

Easton, Penelope S. "A Cheechako Dietary Consultant." *Journal of the American Dietetic Association*, no. 9 (1950): 688-692.

Easton, Penelope S. *Food Resources of Alaska*. Alaska Department of Health, 1950.

Easton, Penelope S. PhD, RD. "Food Considerations for Iditarod Drivers." In *The Iditarod Arctic Sports Medicine/Human Performance Guide*, edited by A. Allan Turner. Anchorage: American College of Sports Medicine, 1989.

Feeney, Robert. E. *Polar Journeys*. Washington and Fairbanks: American Chemical Society and University of Alaska Press, 1997.

Fish. Cooperative Extension Work in Agriculture and Home Economics Extension Service, University of Alaska, 1948.

The Hunter Returns With The Kill. Cooperative Extension Work in Agriculture and Home Economics Extension Service, University of Alaska, 1948.

Kohlhoff, Dean. *When the Wind Was a River*. Seattle: University of Washington Press, 1995.

Kawagley, A. Oscar. *A Yupiaq Worldview*. Prospect Heights: Waveland Press, 1995.

Langdon, Stephen J. and Aaron Leggett. "Dena'ina Heritage and Representation in Anchorage: A Collaborative Project." In *The Alaska Native Reader*, edited by Maria Shaa Tláa Williams, 163–175. Durham: Duke University Press, 2009.

McClanahan, Alexandra J. *Growing Up Native In Alaska.* Anchorage: The CIRI Foundation, 2000.

Sherman, Henry C., PhD, ScD. *Chemistry of Food and Nutrition.* New York: MacMillan, 1937.

Smith, Janell, and Dennis Wiedman. "Fat Content of South Florida Indian Frybread: Health Implications for a Pervasive Native-American Food." *Journal of the American Dietetic Association,* no. 5 (2001): 582–585.

Smith, Janell, Paulette Johnson, Penelope Easton, Dennis Wiedman, and Emma G. Widmark. "Food Customs Of Alaska Women of Childbearing Age: The Alaska WIC Healthy Moms Survey." *Journal of Ecology of Food and Nutrition,* no. 6 (2008): 465–517.

Smith, Janell, Penelope S. Easton, and Brian L. Saylor. "Inupiaq Elders Study: Aspects of Aging Among Male and Female Elders." *International Journal of Circumpolar Health,* no. 2 (2009): 18.

Williams, Maria Shaa Tláa. "A Brief History of Native Solidarity." In *The Alaska Native Reader,* edited by Maria Shaa Tláa Williams, 202–16. Durham: Duke University Press, 2009.

Acknowledgments

Without Janell Smith there would be no ending to this book. There would likely be no book at all. She has been contributor, memory prompter, and fact checker from the beginning. Janell, some years after taking my graduate course in public health nutrition, which included grant writing and field research methods, enhanced her skills and methods when she worked in Alaska with WIC programs and for the University of Alaska at Anchorage. She was courageous enough to later include me, by then a senior citizen, on four of her grant-funded research projects. My only regret is that I cannot go back and raise her grade from B+ to A.

Jo Barbara Taylor is my writing coach and freelance editor. She challenges me to refine my writing and retain my authentic voice. She is also guardian of commas and unnecessary adverbs. Jo is an award-winning poet and retired high school English teacher, and she leads poetry-writing workshops and designs publications. Jo's patience with my frequent changes in direction makes her a valuable collaborator; her computer skills balance my challenged ones and make this book presentable.

My nephew, Frank Easton, is my number one cheerleader. He has spent countless hours editing photographs and advising me in dealing with the publishing process.

Jim Shuping has saved my pictures from old films and slides and rescued me when my computer and I had serious troubles. He is always on call and greatly appreciated.

My family is a network of caring, supportive people: Penny and Ron Manasco, their children, Travis, Garrett, and Allie; Morgan Kupsinel and her children, Easton and Garth; and my cousin Ruth Donnocker.

The Forest at Duke community, Lorraine Clark, Carol and Dick DeCamp, Beth and Tom Everly, Carol Griffith, Peg Lewis, and other friends have submitted to questionnaires about their Alaska trips, read drafts, and offered encouragement.

I am grateful to Mary Elizabeth Braun, acquisitions editor at Oregon State University Press, for her mentoring and faith in the early versions of *Learning to Like Muktuk*; to Micki Reaman, editorial, design, and production manager, for her skill and guidance; and to the OSU Press staff for their expertise and interest.

I have tried to locate some of the Alaskans who are mentioned in this book, especially the public health nurses who taught me so much and made my journey exciting. I tried to find our unit secretary, Mary Davis, who made it possible for me to have the documents I have used to write this book. I hope they, or some of their family members, know how much I appreciate their contributions to my Alaskan experience.

Index